Content Marketing Book: 3 Manuscripts in 1

Easy and Inexpensive Content Marketing Strategies to Make a Huge Impact on Your Business

Copyright 2018 by Eric J Scott – All rights reserved.

This document is geared toward providing exact and reliable information in regard to the topic and issue covered. The publication is sold with the idea that the publisher is not required to render accounting, officially permitted, or otherwise, qualified services. If advice is necessary, legal or professional, a practiced individual in the profession should be ordered.

– From a Declaration of Principles which was accepted and approved equally by a Committee of the American Bar Association and a Committee of Publishers and Associations.

In no way is it legal to reproduce, duplicate, or transmit any part of this document in either electronic means or in printed format. Recording of this publication is strictly prohibited and any storage of this document is not allowed unless with written permission from the publisher. All rights reserved.

The information provided herein is stated to be truthful and consistent, in that any liability, in terms of inattention or otherwise, by any usage or abuse of any policies, processes, or directions contained within is the solitary and utter responsibility of the recipient reader. Under no circumstances will any legal responsibility or blame be held against the publisher for any reparation, damages, or monetary loss due to the information herein, either directly or indirectly.

Respective authors own all copyrights not held by the publisher.

The information herein is offered for informational purposes solely, and is universal as so. The presentation of the information is without contract or any type of guarantee assurance.

The trademarks that are used are without any consent, and the publication of the trademark is without permission or backing by the trademark owner. All trademarks and brands within this book are for clarifying purposes only and are owned by the owners themselves, not affiliated with this document.

Table of Contents

Content Marketing
A Beginner's Guide to Dominating the Market with Content Marketing

Introduction xi

   Chapter 1
   What is Content Marketing? 1

   Chapter 2
   The Importance of Consistent and High-Quality Content 7

   Chapter 3
   Know Your Audience 23

   Chapter 4
   Blogging 32

   Chapter 5
   What You Should Not Overlook 45

   Chapter 6
   Case Studies & Strategies 61

Conclusion 73

Content Marketing
Strategies to Capture and Engage Your Audience, While Quickly Building an Authority

Introduction 77

Chapter 1
Follow Your Passion and Popular Trends 79

Chapter 2
Understand Your Audience 91

Chapter 3
Quality Checklist 103

Chapter 4
Expand Your Horizons... 111

Chapter 5
How to be Prominent on Social Media 133

Conclusion 155

Content Marketing
Tips + Tricks to Increase Credibility

Introduction... 159

Chapter 1
Website Framework... 161

Chapter 2
Your Content..171

Chapter 3
Social Media.. 195

Chapter 4
Expand Your Horizons... 199

Chapter 5
The Value of Listening to Your Audience 209

Chapter 6
Personal Advancement 231

Table of Contents

Conclusion.. 239

Content Marketing

A Beginner's Guide to Dominating the
Market with Content Marketing

Introduction

I want to thank you and congratulate you for downloading the book, "Content Marketing: A Beginner's Guide to Dominating the Market with Content Marketing."

This book contains important details on how best to position your business, improve your reputation and brand to attract a wider audience, and realize a rapid business growth.

You will discover that to succeed and effectively dominate your industry, there must be a shift in your mindset and the processes that you utilize to execute your strategies and related tasks. Your foundation must be flexible enough to withstand challenges, yet sturdy enough to maintain the structures and systems that you will implement to construct a profitable and successful business.

We will focus on innovative approaches, tools, and resources that you should utilize in every phase of your content marketing journey. Whether you only have an idea, or you've already started a business, I have highlighted the essential factors that you should consider as you step into the sphere of content marketing and advance as a leader in your respective industry.

Thanks again for downloading this book. I hope you enjoy it.

Chapter 1

What is Content Marketing?

Content is what you use to communicate with your potential customers or existing customers. It includes your pages on your website, your social media channel, blogs, PowerPoint presentations, newsletters, podcasts, and videos.

Though you may be considering all the work you have to do and have started brainstorming, my objective is to keep you focused on what is important. Before we venture on, you must first know what your goal is. Why, you may ask? Because the content should be used as a tool to support your goals. To help you fine-tune your goals, here are some questions to consider: Do you need to develop an email lists? Do you want more viewers to become customers? Do you wish to keep your customers and encourage them to spend more? Once you know what your goals are, you will know if the content you have created is relevant and will meet your objectives.

Content marketing is using "content" to realize your business marketing goal. Content marketing is more than providing information to an audience with the goal of acquiring profits and acquiring a loyal fan base. These are certain factors you must understand:

•   You should have a strategic plan in order to be effective. Planning will take time. It is not something that you should do in haste and when you are not focused. Also, you will have to track your goals and evaluate your progress to know when they will need to be modified. You should have various steps outlined that will take you from the first step until you have arrived at your desired target.

•   You have to market your content. You cannot create the content, use one medium, and expect the people who use other online resources to know about it just because you have used your preferred medium. You have to showcase your content before an audience.

•   Your content must be high-quality and very informative. Do not have the mindset that fluff and "anything goes" can give you mileage. There is so much information at the fingertips of people around the world and they only gravitate to content that is educational, informative, entertaining, and inspirational.

•   You must have regular content, not the occasional informational post here and there when you are in the mood to create it. Previously, businesses had the say in what to convey and when to communicate with the public.

That has changed as people all over the world have various preferences and various options at the click of a button.
- As already highlighted, your content should help you to achieve your goals.
- When creating content, focus on your specific audience.

Paradigm Shift

You are quite aware what it is like to have conversations with self-centered people. You can pick a neutral topic yet they will always find a way to shine the spotlight on themselves. You can simply be talking about the rainy weather, hoping for conversation, and it will be turned into a monologue. For the talker, it is a wonderful experience. On the other hand, it is not a good experience for the listener.

Similarly, the content that you are creating is not about your business or about you. Your content should not be the opportunity to be self-centered. It is not your brochure or company manual dissected in different parts and you expect the public to be versed on every detail that happened to you and your business. If your audience wants to buy the skin cream that you are advertising, for example, why do you have to mention immaterial and irrelevant details that will not improve their buying experience or make them more informed about the product?

You must realize that the content you are creating is about your audience. You are providing information that will enlighten them, make their lifestyle much easier, eliminate stressful situations in their life, and make them happy and feel like they are connected to a source that adds value to their lives. Your content should be newsworthy, express an opinion about something, offer insights, and be informative.

Differences

Content marketing is not advertising
Content marketing is not advertising, which is a type of structured communication. Advertising focuses on obtaining money quickly. You may turn the pages of a newspaper and see: SALE! SALE! SALE! Buy one get the other ½ price while stock lasts.

With advertising, you are paying a third party to use their medium to capture an audience. In the example given, a business has paid the newspaper an advertising fee to showcase what is being offered. The business will capture the attention of the newspaper's readers. Similarly, it is like going to an event to have an opportunity to see and engage various artists, but you have to pay at the entrance. You do not have access unless you pay.

Content marketing is about producing content to build your own audience. You can use social media, websites, and even pay for advertising, as that is one channel to market your content. However, content marketing is about establishing your own audience.

Think of advertising as waving to someone from across the street and content marketing as not only waving but stopping to engage in conversation and genuinely inquiring how the individual is doing.

Content Marketing is not Public Relations
Public Relations is about the relationship between an organization and the public. There is a difference with PR and Content Marketing also. Content marketing is used daily to engage your audience. PR is usually utilized when there is a special event or negative occasion that needs to be resolved. PR releases are formal and geared around the brand and the message the company wishes to convey to the public. Public relations can be expensive. Content marketing is based on the consumer and can be done in-house, and even if it is outsourced, the costs are affordable. There are parallels, but there is still a distinction.

Content Marketing is not Social Media
Content marketing is about your customers absorbing the knowledge you create, whereas social media is more about sharing that knowledge. Social media is used to distribute your content.

Advertising, Public Relations and Social Media are the promotional avenues that you can use to market your content. However, note the differences so you can create an effective content marketing strategy.

Chapter 2

The Importance of Consistent and High-Quality Content

Long ago, you had to be in a library or educational facility to obtain specific information. Later on, you had to have a computer and the internet to have access to certain information. Today, with just one click of a button on a phone or other mobile device, anyone can access information that used to only be housed in encyclopedias and library reference books.

We do not have to be stationary at the computer to surf the internet. We can check and read material whenever and wherever we may go. With so much information available to people around the world, you have to ensure that the content you produce is more valuable than that of your competitors.

Brand Awareness
The members of your audience have their own habits. Perhaps they have been loyal to your competitors. However, with your content you can get them to change their habits in alignment with your goals. Having quality content strategically positions your brand before an audience. The more they see your brand, the more they can recognize it.

Have you ever walked or driven along a certain route for months or even years, then one day someone points something out to you, which you had never seen before? Then all of a sudden you to start to spot the same thing in various places and enjoy it, when before it was non-existent to you. Or have you ever been introduced to someone and thereafter you spot the individual very frequently? It is the same thing with brand awareness.

Creating content will ensure that your audience has something to talk about. When people include your business in their conversation, they teach and inform other people who may not have been aware of your brand or about your product or service.

Content Marketing Makes You a Reliable and Authoritative Source

The more regularly you create quality content, the more you will be viewed as a reliable and credible source. It is not about quantity. It is not about how much you produce, but what you have produced that can distinguish you from your competitors. Your audience will grow to respect and highly regard your work.

It Captures Audience Attention

Have you ever been offered a sample of a food item that is so tasty that you not only take a second helping but you want to know about the chef? It is the same way when you have quality content. The more remarkable your content, the more you will have people returning to read, see, or hear what you have created.

Increase in Traffic

The more powerful content you create, the more it will enhance your website traffic and search engine optimization (SEO).

Search engine optimization is a way to obtain traffic from search results. Webpages and content on your pages are displayed and ranked according to what the search engines find to be appropriate. For example, if a tourist stops you in the street and asks you to tell him the best place to get a meal, preferably something cheap and in walking distance, you won't send him to a fancy upscale restaurant in a far and remote location. Likewise, if someone looks for a specific topic in search engines, he or she will be given a list of information that is more relevant. The better your content, the more highly it will be ranked and noticed by viewers.

Website Terms and Information

Links
An inbound link refers to a hyperlink that is on another site and leads back to you. An inbound link is sometimes called a backlink.

For example, if you are having an event, you will advertise it in your business place. You may also ask businesses to advertise your event and they may give out flyers to their customers. Individuals reading the flyer will know that you exist and will know more about your business. If this was online, then the business will provide links to your website so people can click the link and be directed to your website.

When you have a lot of inbound links, search engines will rank your page higher on the list. Inbound links is referred to as off-page search engine optimization.

On-page search engine optimization involves positioning keywords within your headlines, subheadings, tags, body content and links. Use a main keyword for each page. Do not use many keywords. Insert your keywords in your headings and subheadings. Also, place them in the content of your body, but don't overdo it.

Bear in mind that though you wish to rank well in the search engines, you are writing for your audience. Thus, ensure that you strike an appropriate balance. Your audience is your first priority.

Meta tag

Meta tag is a code used for search engines to ascertain what your site is about. Most websites have a management system for you to edit meta tags without you having to be an expert in coding, so don't worry. With the advancement of technology, resources are provided for you to make your work much easier. However, you should know what a meta tag is. The objective of the meta tag is to describe your web page for the systems that collect web data. You may have seen it but do not know what it is. Let us assume that a website is called Marketing Software. It may look something like this for a title:

<title>Marketing Software</title>

The description may look like this:

<meta name= "Description" content= "be more engaging, be more appealing. Marketing Software...">

This is just the code for the system. You do not need to be versed in coding for you to be a great content marketer. It is listed here because perhaps you have seen things that look like this, but you weren't sure about the relevance.

The good news is that many of the resources that allow you to build your site using their platform already have the settings in place. If you are unsure, you can consult with a programmer or website developer.

Redirect your page when necessary

If your website address has changed, make sure that you redirect your page to the right place. For example, if your website was www.example.com and you have changed your address to www.goodexample.com, do what is necessary to redirect your page. When visitors go to www.example.com they will see a message "Page Not Found." They may automatically assume that your business no longer exists, and that means you just lost some potential customers. Therefore, make sure to redirect your page. Your hosting company and the place where you bought your domain will be able to provide information on how to direct your page.

The Do's and Don'ts

Content Creation

General Information

Do ensure that you have a specific objective for the content you create. What do you want your audience to do after reading your content? Are you building your email lists? Do you want them to sign up for something?

Do not use more words than necessary. Focus more on the message. You can also use images to assist with conveying your message.

Do know who your audience is.

Do not use uncommon words that leave your audience clueless. Imagine for a second that you are a scientist and regularly give lectures to scholars and academics. You also have a blog where you talk about gardening. Your content should be completely distinct so that anyone wanting to know about gardening can follow, as opposed to having to use a dictionary to understand the scientific terms you have used.

Web Content Writing Information
If you spot an error on your website, change it immediately.

Do remove your tweets if they have errors.

Ensure that your Facebook page is presentable, once you are using it for marketing purposes. Yes, you can keep it interactive, but ensure that it is devoid of blurred pictures and errors.

Do avoid long paragraphs. Writing on the web is different than print. The attention span for viewers online is shorter than those who opt to read printed material. Therefore, keep your paragraphs short.

If you are unsure of anything, the answer is a click away, so research it. It is better to take the time to do so rather than have errors in your work.

Editing and Grammar

Ensure that you give yourself a break before editing your work. The longer break you have, you will be able to spot the errors quicker when you return to your work. You do not always spot errors while writing. It is when your mind is refreshed that you see things more clearly.

Carefully, read each sentence at a time. Do not speed read, but instead take your time.

Observe what patterns you may have and look to spot them. What are your trouble spots? Do you always confuse their and there? Every time you see these words, take your time to ensure that you have used them correctly.

Change what needs correcting when you spot it, whether it is the structure of a sentence, punctuation, or spelling.

Ensure that you read the entire work at a reasonable speed. Do not rush when checking for errors.

Storytelling Tips
Tell stories that you pique your interest
Sometimes we fall in the trap of trying to convey a story we heard, but it is not communicated with the passion and

gusto of the original storyteller. When you retell it, it may sound dull and boring. You may wonder if you have the skill to tell stories. Yes, you do. The key is to tell something that you are passionate about and not what someone else finds interesting.

Make time and prepare
Preparation is very important when telling stories. Do the proper research and make sure that you have enough information to enhance what you wish to communicate.

Remove insignificant parts
If bits and pieces of your story are irrelevant and drag your story to a halt, instead of merrily moving along, remove it. Determine if you really need that bit of information. If you don't need it, take it out.

Listening Formats
All of the information above applies. If you are speaking, bear these in mind also for your listeners.

Have self-assurance
If you are using audio, podcasts, webinars, and similar formats to tell your story, tell your story with confidence. If you are unsure of what you are conveying and doubtful, it will affect how your listeners view you and digest the information.

Pace yourself
Do not hurry along. Speak slowly and clearly so your listeners can hear you.

Visual
If you are using video content, engage your audience by using eye-contact.

Writing style and voice

Voice
Voice is a way of writing that distinguishes you from other writers. When you call a friend and simply say, "Hello," your friend can detect your voice without you having to identify yourself. It is the same way that your readers can identify you. Though they cannot "hear" you from reading your work, they can read your content and identify with your personality. Perhaps your writing is laced with humor or a touch sarcasm or you are very compassionate. Whatever it may be, your voice is what sets you apart from other writers.

Style
Your style is broader and goes beyond your personality. Let us imagine for a second that you are in line at the supermarket. A friend is behind you, cannot see your face but calls your name confidently and is sure that it is you in the line. Your friend may tell you she identified you by your style. Perhaps you always wear a unique set of earrings, or your hair is styled in a fashionable way or you are flamboyant in your dressing or you like wearing baseball caps. In the same way, a reader can identify you by your style. One way to identify style might be your sentence

structure. Are your sentences long and do they meander across the page to get to the final destination? Or are they short and chirpy? Are your sentences packed with many metaphors and imagery so your readers feel that they were right there with you, seeing exactly what you saw?

Right and wrong pertains to grammar. Style is not a matter of what is right or wrong, but what uniquely is your way of writing.

There are four main writing categories and everyone has a specific style.

1. Expository
In this category, a writer informs the readers about a particular topic or subject. It requires facts and supporting information. It is commonly used in textbooks and this type of writing is logical, organized, and straightforward.

2. Descriptive
The focus is more on describing a character, an event, or a place. The objective is more to entertain the audience with the beauty of words. More adverbs, imagery, figurative language, and adjectives are used in this form of writing.

3. Persuasive
The writer gives reasons and justifies his point of view to convince the reader. Sometimes, things are exaggerated and can even be very dramatic to emotionally influence an audience.

4. Narrative
The writer narrates the story. Depending on the genre, a particular type of sentence structure will be used to build excitement or suspense.

Social Media Writing

Avoid your formal voice
There is a difference when communicating on social media platforms. Social media is not as formal as other forms of communication. It's like socializing, letting your hair down, relaxing your shoulders. Therefore, you have to use your casual voice whether or not you are an executive wearing a business suit.

When you start a conversation with someone, do you use a serious face and sound like you are a politician speaking to government officials? Of course not. Try not to sound like you are at a business convention when using social media.

You should ask questions of those you are communicating with and avoid sounding as if you are in the boardroom. Your social voice should be warm and engaging as if you are talking to a friend.

It doesn't mean that you will break all the grammar rules by using question marks when you should use full stops and abandoning all that you know. Just keep it casual.

Short and simple is better

Social media is not a place to sound like a lecturer giving an academic talk. Do not have 40 paragraphs of text where your audience has to scroll and scroll and scroll and scroll to read what you wish to convey. You can condense your summary if you wish, but keep your longer content for other forums. If you don't, you will lose the interest of your audience. Think about it. When you go to a place to hang out and unwind, do you want to keep talking about the latest business policies and talk in detail about everything that happened on the job and sound as if you have read the company's manual? Or do you inquire about what your friends are doing and keep the conversation entertaining?

If you do have a long form of content, provide the link to where individuals can read it and if you do provide commentary, keep it short. Twitter has 140 characters, so there is a limit on how much you can convey.

Action words

Social media is for socializing, but it doesn't mean that you should forget your business goals and objectives. Encourage your followers to perform some kind of action. Do you want them to click on the link? Do you want them to read the post on your blog and share their views? Is there a video you want them to watch on YouTube?

Personal language

Include the right pronouns. Do not speak in the third person and sound formal. For example, if you are the owner of business called We Deliver, do not post, "The owner of

We Deliver would like to inform the customers..." You can simply say, "I would like to share some exciting news with you..." When you use the pronouns "you" and "I," it sounds more engaging. Write as if you are speaking to one person.

Have fun with punctuation
As said above, although you are on social media, you should not break all the grammatical rules. However, you can still have fun with your communication. You are not writing for a group of business consultants. You are free to capitalize words for emphasis and use more than one exclamation point. For example, you can say, "I have GREAT news!!" You will surely have your followers curious.

Edit
Review your work. You do not want your words to be misconstrued. You can have a friend or associate read your post before you post it. For example, you may have wanted to say, "Do visit We Deliver for all your delivery needs," but in reality, you posted, "Do not visit We Deliver for all your delivery needs." One word can be detrimental.

Tips for writing interesting headlines
- Use numbers
- Include interesting adjectives
- Include words such as What, Why, How and When
- Include an incredible promise. Make sure you fulfill it, though. You want to capture your readers' attention not jeopardize your credibility by making promises you cannot keep.

Using humor
Who does not like to laugh? We all do. One injection of humor can surely brighten anyone's day. Use humor, but don't overdo it. Do not share jokes at the expense of a group of people. It may be funny to you, but it may be misconstrued differently. Save the raunchy jokes for your friends and family and remember the goals of your business. You want to make people laugh, not view you in a negative light.

Topics to write about
The content that you provide must have value to your readers. Here are some examples of what you can write about.

- Offer an analysis of an article on the market
- Provide case studies
- Answer questions that you have received
- Mention dialogue that you've had on social media
- Interviews
- Topics in the news.

Chapter 3

Know Your Audience

Persona Profile

You have to know who you are conveying your message to. You have to create a persona profile, which is a profile of your ideal buyer. Identify important factors about the members of your audience.

These are some questions to assist you:

What are your members' demographics?
What are the facts about your audience? What is the age, gender, and location? If you are already in business with data analytics, you can analyze data from your database or management software system. If you have not set one up as yet, list the key factors of your ideal profile.

What are their decision points?

What would make your audience consider your content? What problem or dilemma or need do they have that would make them consider your source? Do you have a viable solution to their needs and can you help them resolve their problems or point them to resources which they can use?

What are their responsibilities?

You would not know about their individual responsibilities. The responsibilities I am referring to are general responsibilities. Are your customers on a tight budget? Let us imagine, for example, that you provide information on how to stretch a dollar and how to shop for deals. You should in no way expect to think that your audience comprises of millionaires and billionaires. If you want to cater to millionaires and billionaires, then readjust your business goals and change your content accordingly.

What are the characteristics of the members of your audience?
Do they buy fancy cars and private jets, or do they camp out on weekends and enjoy nature? What are their attitudes and opinions?

Content briefs

You will have to create what is known as an editorial brief or content brief. These are the points you must consider when planning your brief.
Fundamentals

- What are your objectives?

Why are you doing this? Is it for popularity or to earn a profit? Do you want to help people or do you want people to know more about your brand? Or both?

- Who are you targeting?

You would have already answered this in your persona profile.

- What key points do you want people to digest?

When you buy medication from the pharmacy, you listen to what is said. If you have to take your medication with food, that will the foremost thing on your mind. You won't take them randomly or on an empty stomach because you have forgotten the instructions. Similarly, what do you want your audience to have on their minds while reading your content? What do you want them to remember?

- What supporting evidence do you have?

If you are informing people about the latest technological device, why should your audience believe you? Have you tried it for yourself? If you offer information about real estate, do you know much about the topic? This is very important, as you want your readers to see you as an authority on the topic and value what you have to say. Therefore, provide supporting evidence.

- What is the tone of voice you will be using?

Funny? Witty? Compassionate? There are many options, but you have to know what will be best for you.

- Execution

To implement your content marketing plan, what budget do you need? What is your timing? Do you have guidelines? What format will you use?

Building on the Fundamentals

Be Confident

Just because you are new to content marketing doesn't mean that you should approach your work with uncertainty. Neither does being confident mean that you should overlook the rules because you think you know everything and you are a magnet for attracting an audience. Being confident means that you are aiming to achieve the most you can achieve with the tools before you. It is a mindset. Once you have the correct mindset, it will reflect in what you do and what you produce.

If you will be working with a group of people to provide your content, inform the group what you aspire to achieve, and also inject that level of confidence within your team members.

Beyond Demographics

What beliefs and behavioral patterns, biases, and dislikes are held by the consumers that you are catering to? Your demographics will show you the age and location, for example, but what about the beliefs of your audience? What causes them to buy? This information is termed "psychographics."

To help you gain a better understanding, if you already have a business, you can conduct interviews with your customers. Include those who may be categorized as your worst customer and also your best customer. You will better understand how your business is viewed by your audience and also what interests them.

Another way to examine this is by using your data. For example, let us imagine that you have a website with health content. You had free giveaways for your topic on diabetes and also on cholesterol. When you check your data, the number of people who opted for the free giveaway about the diabetes topic was three times the number of those who downloaded information on cholesterol. From what the report is showing you, you will realize that more members of your audience are concerned about diabetes or want to know more about it.

If you want to know more, you can also offer surveys on your website for people to give honest feedback. The results can provide you with a better insight as to why your audience will buy a product or gravitate toward a product more than something else.

What do you want your audience to consider?
What do you want your audience to feel after reading your content? If you are producing information on health, do you want them to feel overwhelmed and that they allowed their life to get out of control? Do you reprimand them for

overeating and not exercising? Are you condescending in you tone? Was that your intention, or do you want your audience to feel that it is never too late to begin? Do you want them to feel empowered and that they can do everything that they have set their minds to achieve and you will help them along the way?

Once you have a better understanding of what you wish to achieve, your content will reflect it.

Tell a Story
Outline what angle you will take your story. Don't just create, but strategize what angle is best to achieve your goals. For example, if you owned a health website, you can tell your story about what caused you to start the website. What challenges did you have? What was your wake-up call? How did you achieve your health goals? Your audience will connect with you more knowing that you once struggled and are now triumphant.

Content Producers
You have identified your audience, you have your content brief, what is your next move? It is time to produce your content. You do not have to wait until the end to think about it. However, it is placed here because sometimes when you have already earmarked someone for the job, when you have formalized your strategy, you may realize that the person is not best suited for the role.

For example, in your content brief you may have adjusted a few things and have decided that the end product will focus on fashion designs. Imagine that you have already identified a writer whose specialty is in sports. The content that is produced has more to deal with what athletes are wearing when competing. On the other hand, you were more interested in the latest designs coming out of Europe and what the highly paid models are wearing.

Whereas you were hoping to attract a fashion-conscious audience, because of the content produced by the content producer, you have attracted sports fans. Perhaps that may have been your initial intention, but during the brief you adjusted a few things. It is very important that you know what you hope to achieve and what stepping stones will take you there. That way you can inform the people who will help you with your content so everyone has the same mindset.

Who do you have in mind to write your content or assist you with creating your content? Or do you plan to do everything yourself? It all depends on what your business objectives are. You cannot look at what your competitor is doing, for your competitor's goals would be completely different from yours even though you may be producing the same thing.

Your foundation must be strong, so select your team with care. You can select an agency or hire freelancers to assist you with your content.

Hiring

When hiring, you will have certain qualities and skills that you are looking for. You should look at someone who is enthusiastic and talented rather than someone who is just writing because "it is just a job." What does the person like about writing?

Does the person know about content marketing and have any ancillary skills? Does the person keep deadlines? Does the writer have the ability to multitask?

You can also inquire how the writer determines what topics to write about and what format they would take. This question will give you more insight into the person's thought process and what motivates his or her action. Or perhaps the writer uses data and analytics and recent trends to decide what topic to write on. You would hire someone who can offer suggestions and advice.

Editorial Calendar

Your next step is to organize your priorities. What will you be publishing and when will it be published? Do not take this step for granted. You surely insert your personal events on a calendar as a reminder. Likewise, you have to schedule when you will create your content and what supporting activities are needed to do so.

Do not produce content just for the sake of feeling like you are doing something. Stick to your plan to keep your focus.

Places to Publish Your Content

Your website is where you will start. Think of it as your home base. Then you will distribute your content through various channels including email, YouTube, Twitter, Facebook, LinkedIn and the host of other platforms that are available at your fingertips. Only you can decide what platforms are best for you. However, be open to trying new things and exploring various options.

Content marketing does not involve scrambling to find an audience and then building your content to cater to them. Content marketing is strategic and anything that is well thought out will take time. Building the foundation is not something that can rushed. Once you have invested in content and it is worthy and valuable, the audience will be attracted to your platform.

Chapter 4

Blogging

"Blog" is the shortened name for "web log." It is a log of entries on a website. It can be one where different people are contributors or a blog can be written solely by the owner of the website.

As a blogger, you should be passionate about the topics you choose. If you are enthusiastic about what you doing, it will reflect in your content. The content on your blog is owned by you. You set the rules, unlike other social media platforms where you have to abide by their rules. You can build your audience via social sharing and offering an opportunity to comment.

To ensure that your blog is aligned with your objectives, these are some steps to consider.

Domain Name
If you do not have a website at this point in time, you should consider a domain name. It is the first point of contact with the public. When choosing a domain name,

ensure that it is easy to remember and spell. A website with a name that is hard to pronounce and even harder to spell is not something anyone wants to be bothered with. You can use one of your keywords in your domain name if you unsure of what to use. For example, let us assume you have a business and wish to talk about the various types of fans on the market and there is a brand called Wer which is a brand that is relatively new on the market. However, you like the design. You wish to come up with a name. If viewers see a site thebestfans.com or wer.com, they wouldn't have to wonder what the "thebestfans" site is all about as you have used your keyword "fan" in the domain name.

Hosting and Themes

You have to decide who will host your domain name. Therefore, do your research and see which company's rates are affordable and what they have to offer. Also, decide which platform you will use for your blog. Whose design will you use? There are various sites that offer themes for bloggers, such as WordPress. Decide which one is best for you. If you will use a free theme regardless of which site you will use, ensure that the background, header images, and custom menus are presentable. Make sure you can also have proper data analytics so you can check your data in the future.

The worst possible thing you can do is to have a beautiful blog with all the eye-catching details, but there is no feature for you to access your data. Remember that content marketing is more than eye-catching content. You have to strategize to achieve your goals. Make sure that the blog host has all the necessary resources for you to realize your goal.

You also have the option of paying for premium themes with your respective design company of choice. Make your selection carefully if you do opt for this method rather than using the free themes. If you are paying for something, make sure that you know what you will receive in exchange.

Logo

Do you have a logo? If you don't, you should get one as it helps people with identifying your brand immediately. When hiring a designer, ensure that you convey the correct information about your goals and business objectives. You can ask your friends and family members for suggestions if you are unsure of whether the logo you have chosen conveys the right message. You can also run a competition where various designers create logos and then choose the best one.

Plugins

A plugin is a type of software that gives your website more functionality. There are various plugins for WordPress, and by using them you can add more features to your website. For example, email clients may use a software to encrypt email. One plugin that you are familiar with, is Adobe Flash Player. Sometimes when you go on various websites, you may see a message alerting you that Flash Player needs to be installed or updated.

The Flash Player plugin allows you to see content in a format that will give you a better experience. For example, if you click on a video, you will want to see the video from beginning to end with no complications rather than reloading it every couple of seconds because it keeps stopping. If you are obtaining your plugins from various third party developers, be careful with what you use on your website. How well they operate depends on how well they were developed in the first place. If you are not sure about this leg of the journey, consult someone who knows about websites and plugins.

Writing
What you write about depends on your business objectives. We have already discussed the essentials of writing for your audience. Remember that blogging is one way to strategize. It is not the only way.

Perhaps you may wonder why you should blog. These are reasons why you should embrace it.

A blog improves your search optimization.
Once you are operating from your own domain and not a third party blogging website, by using your keywords and providing links to other web content, you can improve how well your audience finds you when doing a search. Using the example above, if someone wants to know about what brands of fans are popular choices and they do their research in the search engines, the websites that offer reviews and suggestions will appear. Let us assume that the

blogger on the best fans has two years of solid and valuable content with many comments and feedback, so the website will be listed higher in the search engines.

On the other hand, if the domain name is not as strong as it could be, you are using a third-party platform site like www.wer/thirdpartyplatform.com and the site only contains pictures of fans and a brief overview, your ranking will not be as high as the other option where the owner has been continuously blogging about fans.

The blog belongs to you.
Let us examine this scenario. Your name is Nate Myers and you are a photographer. You own a Facebook page where you post adorable photos. Your followers know how to contact you. Since opening your Facebook page, you have seen a steady growth of clients. You are running a contest, many people are taking part, and you will announce the winner in five hours.

All is well... until Facebook shuts down your page for violating one of the company's terms and policies. The last thing you posted was a picture of two adorable puppies playing with a ball and you wonder what in the picture was in violation. You search the photo for clues, yet you cannot figure out what you have done to cause your page to be in question. You contact Facebook contesting the company's claims. Two days later, you reclaim your page with angry followers upset that you didn't post who won the contest.

They are asking if you were scamming them. You have to appease them and find a way to salvage your reputation.

It was after contacting Facebook that you realized there was a mix up. Someone in a different country reported you, but the person made an error. The violator was Nate Mayers. The complainer made a typo and it read Nate Myers. You finally receive the wakeup call that although you have a Facebook account, you are at the whim and mercy of the company's policies and someone else's mistake. Your account can be hacked or shut down at any time, and there is nothing you can do until it is resolved. On the other hand, the content on your blog is owned by you. With your own blog, you do not have to wonder if you will be locked out of your account.

Blogs are a 24-hour source of communication.
You can publish your content at any time when you own a blog. Using the example of being locked out of your Facebook account, during that time you could not communicate with your audience. By having a blog, people from anywhere in the world can view your blog and see who won the contest, rather than wonder what happened when they didn't hear from you.

You can use any format on your blog.
You can use text, videos, charts, PDFs, e-books, whitepapers, audio, PowerPoint presentations, and any other format on your blog. You are not limited. If there are any limitations, it is because your blog was not properly

designed to incorporate certain formats. That is why you must ensure that your blog is properly designed and hosted.

A blog is easy to use.
Anyone can own a blog and be successful once they follow certain guidelines as listed above. You do not need to know about computer programming, nor do you have to be versed in the various forms of software.

A blog is affordable.
Having a blog is very affordable. You do not have to worry about taking a loan to own one.

There are other things to consider if you decide to blog. Here are a few of them:

Administrator
If you are not working alone and you have other contributors, you can determine who you want to be your blog administrator. This person will be responsible for the overall management of the blog. The individual has to market the blog through various avenues on social media platforms, develop the plan, select the target keywords, and know about the latest search engine optimization topics.

Blog Guideline
What is the word length of your posts? Does your blog contribute toward your business goal? What tone will you use? In your blog guidelines, you should answer these

questions so when you sit to write, you keep focused instead of wondering what the next step is. Publication Schedule

You may have the date of publication marked on your editorial calendar, but what about the activities that lead up to the publication date? Having a publication schedule allows you to track your progress. Who will be contributing to your blog? When will the person or persons send you the information? Who will edit what was written? Are there pictures or videos to complement the article? Will you contact a photographer or will you ask your friend who told you she has a lovely picture for your post? Did you send your friend a reminder to look for the picture? Your publication schedule allows you to organize and plan the process.

Give Credit
Though the site belongs to you, if you have other bloggers, give them credit when it is due. You can create a profile of your bloggers with pictures and bios so your audience knows who they are interacting with. If you do not wish to take that route, make sure that your bloggers know that they are appreciated.

After you have written your post...

Check for keywords.
Examine your content and select the topics in your post. Use keyword tools to observe popular terms and phrasing. For example, you can use Google Trends. It shows the

frequency that a search term is entered in the search engine. Based on what you have observed, modify your content accordingly. This can be your content, title, or meta tags.

RSS feed
RSS stands for Rich Site Summary and it is a system for providing frequent web content. It allows anyone who utilizes it to stay up to date on information. It allows anyone to obtain the latest content from your website. If your regular bakery provides your favorite cookies once a week and then they sell them twice a week, you would want to know about it. The bakery may display a sign or have flyers so customers know about it. Likewise, an RSS feed allows an audience to know about updated changes on a website.

Once you have enabled the correct settings on your website, when you publish a post, it is automatically updated to your social networking sites that you are connected with. So rather than publishing on your blog, then signing into Facebook to post, then signing in to other social sites to post, all you need to do is publish once and let the software do the rest.

Look for other related blog posts.
By commenting on other blogs, you can generate traffic to your site, too. Do not be obvious. Remember your content is for adding value to an audience; it's not a sales pitch. Don't comment on someone's blog, "Hi guys, check out my post at thebestfans.com. I have what you are looking for so just

click the link below!!!" Can you imagine posting that on a blog that deals with recipes? If you do, do not be surprised if your comment is deleted or the followers of that blog refer to you as behaving out of line. The aim is to attract an audience, so be mindful of what you do.

Share your post with your target audience.
Share the information with the people who will be interested in your content. Earlier I addressed the demographics and psychographics. Moreover, if you did surveys and questionnaires, you will have more insight on what your audience members are thinking and doing.

Feature your posts in your newsletter.
If you have a newsletter or are thinking of getting one, and you are worried about where to find content, your problem will be solved once you a blogger. You can incorporate headlines and a few sentences to inform your subscribers about the topics on your site.

Have other writers comment your blog post.
Rather than commenting, "Hi guys, check out my post at thebestfans.com. I have what you are looking for so just click the link below," you will gain more mileage if a blogger mentions your post. Let's assume a recipe blogger spent an hour preparing tasty treats. In her post, she comments, "While the cakes were in the oven I took a break and enjoyed the breeze from my x fan. My kitchen is always hot, but thanks to The Best Fans blog, I was able to buy mine at a discount." Readers will want to know about your blog and

what discounts you have to offer. Simply ask several bloggers to mention your post and ensure that you make the right selection. For example, if someone's blog is littered with discriminatory topics and your blog is about equal rights, but you are adamant that the person may want to feature your blog, do not be surprised if when you ask, the blogger wants nothing to do with your blog on justice for all. Be realistic and choose wisely.

Dealing with Trolls

Have you ever enjoyed an article online so much that you scanned the comments, smiling until you read the most insulting comments that totally distract other readers and commenters from the topic? You are only a reader. Can you imagine how the publisher of the content must feel? There are people who have made it their purpose to offend and upset as much as they can on the internet. These people are referred to as trolls.

They initiate arguments, post comments to incite, provoke readers, and go off topic. It is harassment online. Their objective is to disrupt. Some individuals view their comments as sincere and valid contributions. Nonetheless, when you publish content, you will attract individuals who are malicious in their postings.

They hide behind the anonymity of the internet and most of the time they use fake usernames.

What You Should Not Overlook

In the United Kingdom, the Malicious Communications Act 1988 and the Communications Act 2003 addresses this subject matter. Individuals have been imprisoned in the United Kingdom for online harassment.

So how do you deal with trolls?

- You should have a policy on your website and other platforms outlining what type of comments are allowed and those that will not be tolerated.
- Completely ignore them. Trolls vie for attention. Their goal is to get you mad and upset. Do not give in. Do not get angry and lash out at them, for then they have accomplished what they set out to do in the first place.
- Another option is to respond in a lighthearted way. I'm sure in real life, you have smiled at people who have offended you when in fact you feel like screaming. Use experience to withstand the taunting and teasing.
- Take away their power. You do not have to name them and let the world know their identity, but you can find ways to make what they have said insignificant.
- Delete the comments if you have the power to do so. Most websites usually allow you to approve of comments before they are published to the world. When you go through the comments and they are rude and littered with profanity, just delete them.
- You can also ban members if they are known for their disruptive tendencies.
- You can prevent an audience from commenting. The disadvantage with this option is that while you are disabling

one person or a few persons, you are stifling great discussion and dialogue on your blog with the rest of the world. So if you do use this option, be mindful of the long-term effect.

- If you do not have the time, you can hire people to monitor your content when published. So rather than waiting 12 hours later when you actually have the time to check, someone will be able to remove distasteful comments as soon as they appear.
- A community of loyal supporters can take care of trolls without you having to do so. However, they need to be mature and experienced at handling trolls. You do not want your comment feed to be littered with a back and forth series of insults between your loyal supporters and trolls.
- Take the comments into consideration. Sometimes the comments can genuinely be coming from a customer who has had a bad experience. Take the time to read and ascertain whether the comment is valid enough for you to take action.
- Respond with facts. When trolls are spreading wrong information and rumors, rather than wait for the rumors to die, you should answer with the facts right away. You should not want anything controversial hampering the credibility of your product or service.
- If a mistake is highlighted by a troll, make the correction and you can admit that you were wrong. You can inform the person that you have made the corrections.

Chapter 5

What You Should Not Overlook

Avoid using the third person
Do you remember that one teacher in high school that no matter how interesting a topic was, they made it boring with their tone? It was enough to make you fall asleep. There are also fond memories of those teachers who can take any topic and make it so entertaining that you were sorry when the class was over. It had to do with their teaching style.

Similarly, ensure that your writing style is like your favorite teacher's approach to imparting knowledge to students. You may not realize it, but using the third person is perceived by your audience as very formal and uninteresting.

Imagine there are two companies who were awarded for their sterling contribution for their fund-raising activities in the community. You read this on one website: Wildflower

Corporation was honored at the mayor's gala. Then you go to another website and see this: Hooray! Guess what? We received an award at the mayor's gala just a few hours ago and we couldn't have done it without your support. Thank you! The first one sounds very detached, as if the company is reporting about another company instead of its own. Do not be robotic while writing.

Do not neglect to use visuals.
Pictures, videos, and PowerPoint presentations can all be used to convey your message. Your content will be more appealing, so use them.

Know the profile of your audience.
Do not downplay your demographics and psychographics. Do not pay the least attention to your personal profile and related activities.

Share your content.
Do not focus so much on blogging that you overlook other platforms where you can place your content. Content marketing is more than blogging. Blogging is a channel to distribute your content. Do not, however, focus 99% of your time on blogging and 1% on other forums.

When you do blog, remember to share what you have written. Sharing is more than spending five seconds to post it in a forum. You have to strategically think of where you will share your content. What are your goals? What do you want? Where is your audience? For example, if your website is based on gardening resources and there are various gardening groups on Facebook, sign up and share your information. Sharing your content with a Facebook group that is more interested in fashion will not give you your desired outcome. Therefore, plan properly.

40 Questions and Answers

1.   Is your headline straightforward and on target?
If your headline is more than 55 characters, you stand the chance of it being chopped off on the search results in Google. You have to be creative in crafting your headline. Will your audience know what you are conveying, or do they have to read the entire article to understand your message? If people are unsure before they click on a link, they will move right along to another page or platform.

2.   Is your topic something that someone will type in the search engines?
For example, let's assume you wrote an article on how to get over a hangover quickly, and you post it around the holidays. It is a topic people will want to know more about as around the festive season people overindulge. On the other hand, if you wrote an article where you reminisce about Easter in the middle of the Christmas Holidays, you will not get as many hits as topics that are relevant to Christmas and the New Year.

3.   Is your headline interesting?

Does your headline make your audience want to click immediately? Do you have popular keywords and phrases in your headline? If your headline is not as interesting as it can be, it will not rank significantly well in Google and other search engines.

4.   Is the introduction of your blog engaging?

If your readers are hooked in the middle of the blog instead from the beginning, you will have to consider rewording your introduction or shifting your paragraph. Not everyone will read on, and you will lose a significant amount of readers if they find your introduction dull. Make sure that your introduction piques their curiosity and makes them want to read more.

5.   Is the body of your content short and sweet or longwinded?

To delve into the body of your content, make sure that there are few paragraphs between the introduction and the body of content. If the reader is only digesting the meat of your content after ten long paragraphs, then you have surely missed the mark. Therefore, condense, reword, and restructure.

6.   Did you include any visuals in your blog post?

You can never go wrong by including a picture or video in your blog post. We are in the era where people expect to see pictures and videos. If your blog post is just text, some of your readers may click over to another website that provides visuals. Think of it this way—if a friend tells you about her wonderful vacation and the beautiful scenery at the destination, would you want to see the pictures as well, or is hearing the details enough?

7. Does your content have subheadings?
It is your preference whether you want to use subheadings or not. However, remember that the content is for the audience and not for you. Subheadings make it easier for readers to navigate their way through your article.

8. Are you using the correct amount of lines for a paragraph on the blog?
Remember it is not a book you are writing, a manual, whitepaper, or magazine. Six lines is acceptable. If you do opt to use more lines, keep your sentences short.

9. Is your tone conversational?
Use "you" and "I" in your content to make it more personal and conversational.

10. What other way can you make your content conversational?
You can italicize your questions. It gives an appearance that you are more personable.

11. Are you making your content more attractive?
You should use any tool that will enhance your content. Examples of useful tools includes audio, video, charts, and images.

12.   Is your content filled with substance or fluff?

You do know what it is like to buy that bag of your favorite potato chip. You open it and the air escapes and you are left with ¼ of what you initially thought was in the bag. Don't you feel absolutely cheated? In the same way, you should not have content that is full of fluff. As was emphasized from the beginning, create content that is of value.

13.   Are you using the correct vocabulary?

Do readers have to have a dictionary close by to read your content? Do they also need to reference an encyclopedia to understand certain terms? Do not use words that will cause you to lose your audience. Make sure that the people you have hired to write your content are experienced enough to know the right wording for your audience.

14.   Is your post formatted properly?

Did you use bulleted points and other features properly? Make the reading experience easier for your audience. Take the time to format your content correctly.

15.   Did you include authority figures in your blog post?

You should include quotes from the experts to make your content more reliable. If, for example, your content is predominantly about diabetes, where did you source your information? Did you quote what doctors and experts have said?

16.   Did you provide supporting facts?
If you make a claim, it is always best to provide facts to support your claim. You can use charts and statistics and similar resources. The last thing you would want is in the middle of reading your post, someone leaves your website to open a browser to find proof of what you have claimed. In the interim, the reader may forget to return to your post as his or her interest has shifted.

17.   At the end of your blog post, do you have a summary?
A nice summary should be 150 words or 200, if you need extra words. If your summary is 500 words, then it may be construed as rambling. If you find you have a lot to say in the summary, you need to restructure your post. Perhaps you need to include another paragraph and not pack everything in the summary.

18.   Do you have a way to collect emails?
You should have a system in place to obtain your audience emails. You can incorporate a lead magnet which is something that persuades people to sign up. For example, you can offer something for free, once they sign up.

19.   Is it really that important to share content on other platforms when I have a blog?
Yes. A blog is but one way to share your content. Perhaps you are not really a sociable person and haven't quite gotten the hand of other platforms. You can hire someone to assist you just as you have other people to help you with your

content. How will people find you if they do not know about you? Blogging is one way, but not the only way, to share your information.

20. Does your post have social sharing buttons?
You should have social sharing buttons so that your audience can also share the content with their friends and associates. There is nothing wrong with asking your audience to share what you have published.

21. Did you use expert sources in your sharing platform?
You should mention your sources for others to share. I am not referring to just in your content but in the format where others can share. For example, you can tweet, "Eating more of x lowers your cholesterol." You may give your food item and set it up so others can retweet it. Let's suppose that in your research, you discovered that Jim Jones, a celebrity, ate the same food item and it improved his health. Jim Jones now has his own show and radio broadcast advocating for the use of the food item. Doctors have confirmed what Jim Jones is saying is correct. One of the doctors is highly respected in his field and has received many awards. Jim Jones is now the rave on the media. People all across the world are talking about Jim Jones. Isn't that the perfect opportunity to include what Jim Jones and doctors are saying, for it to be shared? It surely is. A tweet or Facebook post will surely be shared more times by you referencing Jim Jones and the doctor than if you neglect to include the information.

22. Have you shared your content more than once?

You should share it more than once so that your users will see it. Be mindful that your tweet or other sharing avenue has to compete with tweets and posts from people commenting on the same topic. You have to ensure that your content is visible.

23. Do you need to create new content all the time?

No. What you can do is rework your content. This means that you create content in one format and then use the same information in other forms. For example, your topic is on gardening and you wrote an article about it. You can use the same topic but make it more interactive by doing a video of you or a friend gardening and showing exactly how to do certain things. Perhaps you have pictures of how dilapidated your yard once looked compared to how it looks now. You can feature a photo gallery to highlight what you've implemented and showcase how your flowers are now blooming. It is the same information, but you have used various formats. Moreover, this allows the same content to be digested by people who have different preferences. Individuals who prefer reading will appreciate your post. People more inclined to visuals will prefer the pictures and videos. Those who prefer more interaction will prefer the video. All you have to do is be creative with how you rework your content.

24.   How often should you publish fresh content?
It depends on the business you are in. Ideally twice a week can suffice. If you post more often, that is remarkable too. However, it is better to have value and quality rather than quantity. If you do post every day, ensure that your content has substance to it. Do not post just because everyone is doing it. Other people's goals will be quite different from yours.

25.   Do you really need an editorial calendar?
I highlighted this before, and if you are just starting your business perhaps you may wonder if it applies to you or a big company only. Everything is dependent on your strategy. An editorial calendar is a resource that will keep you more organized and focused on your goals. Do not overlook its importance.

26.   What is evergreen content?
Evergreen refers to plants that retain green leaves no matter what the season. Evergreen content is information that stays relevant and fresh despite what is happening. Evergreen content means that long after you have posted your content, it remains important. It does not include the latest trends and fashionable clothing designs, articles on pop culture, articles about the season as they would only be relevant at a particular season, articles about what is happening in the news, and reports on statistics and data.

Evergreen formats include tips, lists, "how to" instructions, and videos. Just because you use these formats doesn't mean that your content will automatically be classed as evergreen. For example, if you do a video highlighting tips on how decorate your home at Christmas, the content is seasonal. However, if you create a video with the topic, "Tips to de-clutter your home," that is a topic that can be discussed all year round.

27. Is short content or long content better?

Remember we spoke about the length of the paragraphs on your blog post. However, depending on other forms of content, only you can decide what is best for your audience. For example, if you offer ebooks and PDFs, you may prefer to have brief information or you may decide to have a lot of information. It all depends on your audience. You can provide the various options on your website and see what your audience prefers.

28. What types of content are more successful?

Vary your content. You will not know what is better for your business and your audience unless you test the market. For example, an expert in the industry may say webinars are better but that data may be dependent on what works for that particular expert in his specific industry. Perhaps from the data analytics of the company, their audience was more appreciative of webinars. However, it may not be the same for your audience. The only way to know what is best for you is to offer various content and after analyzing your data, you will know what is best for you.

29.   What tone should you use?

You should use the tone that your audience prefers and what will enhance your brand. If your website is about relationships, a formal tone will not be appropriate. The topics discussed in Chapter 3 will assist you.

30.   Where can I get inspiration for content?

Inspiration can be found on blogs that you enjoy reading. What are your competitors posting? You can approach it from the same and also a different angle. Engage in brainstorming more often. Engage your customers and customer support team. Refer to websites that you like. You can also get inspiration from the comments on your posts.

31.   How do I know what my audience values?

Ensure that you have a format for your audience to comment and continue the dialogue. With the email addresses which you have collected, you can send out questionnaires requesting that they select the topics they want to know more about. Furthermore, you can also conduct a poll on your website.

32.   Do you really need to hire experienced writers when others can create valuable content, too?

You cannot substitute experience with anything else. You are competing with other brands—not just in your locale, but globally. Think long-term instead of short-term. You will receive what you have paid for. If you want quality, hire those who will give you better quality than what others are offering.

33.   If someone asks you to define your content, what should you say?
Your content should be mission-driven. What is your mission? Once you can talk about your mission, then you will know how best to define your content.

34.   Should you ask other people to use their platform to share your content?
Yes, you should do so. Know who you will link with to ensure that your content is appropriate. When you have published your post, you can email other sites and ask them to share on their social platforms, too.

35.   How important is using current events?
Though you may use evergreen topics, depending on your subject, you will need to identify trends and include them in your content. One sure way to increase traffic is to have content about a topic that is trending. For example, if your blog caters to sports yet you failed to mention anything about the Olympics, that is one huge error.

36.   How significant are keywords?
Though you are writing for an audience, you should also be mindful that keywords help you to improve your ranking. Do not overlook them. Using the example above, with billions of people keying in the word Olympics 2016 in the search engines, many of the sites who have included that keyword have seen an improvement in traffic.

37. Is guest blogging necessary?

Guest blogging, though it is not mandatory, is a vital marketing strategy that you should consider. Content is content whether it appears on your website or someone else's website. The same rules apply. If you invite someone to blog on your website, ensure that the content has value and vice versa.

38. Should you outsource or handle content production in-house?

It depends on your resources and time. That is why you have to strategize and plan properly. You may have the capabilities to create content, but what other work-related and personal matters do you have on your calendar? Be realistic. If you know that you will not be able to create quality work, then hire someone or a team to do so.

39. What is a common mistake?

Writing content that sounds like it was penned by a showy salesman is a very common mistake to make. That is why it is important to focus on your objectives and plan properly before you start writing. It is not about you, but your audience. A sales pitch will not be deemed as valuable by your audience.

40. How can you measure the success of your efforts?

One method to measure your success is by the number of conversions produced. However, do not look at your present data and think that it is a one-time process. If you posted information and your data shows that 800 people read your post but only 3 bought the item, do not be disappointed. Content marketing is a relationship. You have to keep producing content, not stop when you have just begun. A visitor may read the blog and only after reading several posts weeks later, decide to buy your product. Therefore, give your marketing efforts time, for surely they will pay off and you will reap the benefits.

Chapter 6

Case Studies & Strategies

Huffington Post

The Huffington Post was launched in 2005 and provides the public with news ranging from politics to technology and entertainment and women's interests. In 2012, out of the 15 most popular political sites, it was ranked as #1 by ebizMBA Rank. Moreover, that same year it obtained a Pulitzer Prize.

One of the co-founders, Arianna Huffington, who was born in Greece, ran as an independent candidate for governor in the California recall election in 2003. She did not win, but six years later, in 2009, she was referred to as one of the Most Influential Women in Media. Huffington Post's other co-founders are Ken Lerer and Jonah Peretti.

In 2011, AOL, America Online, acquired the Huffington Post and Arianna became the President and Editor-in-

Chief. In August 2016, she announced that she was leaving her position at the Post, moving on and starting her own company which would focus on wellness.

There are local editions and international editions. The local version was first launched in Chicago in 2007. Thereafter, one was launched in New York followed by Denver, Los Angeles, San Francisco, Detroit, Miami, and Hawaii. There are international editions in various countries, also.

Today the Post is a dominant online news source. It was first a political blog, but now provides readers with a variety of topics such as college life, technology, world news, living, business, and entertainment. The key is the people who are producing their content.

If Huffington Post's content was boring and offered little value, they would not have become a giant in the industry today. They have more than 3,000 contributing bloggers. These contributors include celebrities, academics, and politicians.

Since they started years ago, technology has surely changed, but they have kept abreast and adjusted accordingly.

Last year Huffington Post implemented videos, demonstrating how to make certain dishes to their Facebook fans in 60 seconds or less. For people who are too busy, this simple and time saving technique really appealed to them. This may not seem like a big deal, but Huffington Post was established before Facebook. Adam Denenberg, the Vice President of Engineering, has expressed in several interviews that his goal was to ensure that the online news source was ready for the influx of users as individuals were accessing content from their mobile devices more than their desktop computers. He focused on a modernized platform to adapt to the change in technology.

He had to ensure that the platform could handle the amount of traffic. Moreover, he had to choose the right software to maximize productivity for their editors. They have the appropriate software where editors from different locations can log on and edit the work without emailing back and forth or using a third-party system.

Lessons
Choose the people who will produce your content very carefully. Huffington Post's bloggers are experts in their respective fields. Just because you are just starting out doesn't mean that you should hire anyone you can find or those whose rates are the cheapest. You need remarkable content. What you do today will reflect on how well you maintain your position in the future.

Ensure that your platform can handle the traffic when it arrives. Moreover, determine how you will interact with your content creation team. Rather than emailing back and forth, you can use a platform where anyone can log on and review or edit a document to save time. Though you need the right editors and writers, they must be also be versed in technology. Can you imagine if you used an editor who insisted on faxing certain information to you rather then emailing? Thus, when scouting for members of your team, consider also how individuals will increase productivity.

Birchbox
Birchbox is based in New York and was launched in 2010 by two graduates from Harvard Business School. It is an online subscription service where subscribers receive samples of makeup and beauty products.

When Birchbox first started, they had 600 subscribers. Now there are over one million subscribers and almost 1000 brand partners. They rely on surveys to garner information about the subscribers.

The company has videos on personal grooming. Very frequently subscribers can access grooming videos for both men and women. It is one thing to read about grooming, but Birchbox has taken it to another level by capitalizing on visuals. The company values its customers by showing them how to look their best. Today they are in more than five countries.

Lessons
Mutual benefit is a key component when strategizing. The company's model is based on sending other companies' products to consumers. If you receive free products and try it and realize how awesome it is, won't you continue using

it? Of course you will. This opens up avenue for the manufacturers of the products. Additionally, Birchbox also provides the content about the product. This is a win situation for the manufacturer, in exchange for sending free samples. Consumers can also give their reviews about a product on Birchbox's website.

Content marketing is about interacting with your consumers. Remember, it is about the customers.

Home Depot

The objective of the founders of the Home Depot which started in 1978 was to build superstores that were dedicated to home improvement. The content they provide helps consumers in their everyday lives. For example, they share content on how to save energy or tips on selecting certain items for the holidays such as Christmas trees.

Additionally, the company has YouTube videos with information about home improvements. They not only tell you, but also show you what to do. On Twitter, they also continue with the discussion about decorating and repairs.

The Apron is the name of Home Depot's blog. Their in-store employees add content to the blog. This is an innovative form of content generation, and it also saved the company money by using associates who have the knowledge to communicate what they know to a wider audience. The company will know who is best to write the content, but it adds a bit of personal touch.

Lesson

Your content can answer questions that consumers have. Do not just think short-term but also long-term. Consumers will have questions and concerns about the upcoming holidays. You do not have to wait until consumers email a question. In our previous illustration, we used the example of someone who has a health blog. You do not have to wait until someone inquires if you have any recipes to share with diabetics. You can think ahead and have information for your users. If your competitor offers the same health topics but also provides recipes, tips, and more information, the audience will gravitate to your competitor's website.

Additionally, using associates to add to content is one way of cementing Home Depot's authority and credibility in the business. An associate who has hands-on experience, who customers know, as opposed to someone who is doing research behind the scenes, adds a personal touch.

The videos help to bridge the gap between the business and consumers. No one is in designer suits talking about home products. Customers see people who look like them who want the best for their money. They can relate to what is being said.

When creating videos, make sure that your attire correlates to your product and overall brand.

Alcatel-Lucent
Alcatel and Lucent Technologies was founded 1872 and 1870 respectively. They produce hardware, software, and telecommunications services. In 2006 they merged and in 2016 the company was acquired by Nokia.

Before being acquired by Nokia, the company launched "The New Guy" campaign. It was a series of sitcom-style videos focusing on customers' problems and thereafter they provided engaging ebooks giving solutions and capturing the consumers' attention. The e-books contained a question and answer format. The sitcom series obtained 600,000 views. This creative campaign was the company's most viewed promotion.

The videos and the e-books had none of the technical jargon that often overwhelms consumers.

Lessons
Keep your messages simple. Do not use language that frustrates your consumers. Instances where you have to use technical or scientific explanation, ensure that it is written in such a way that your audience understands.
This is a wonderful example of how the company used humor to captivate its audience. The videos and e-books were educational, but the injection of humor kept people entertained.

Strategies to implement

Have a support group
Invite a group to support and interact with your content. For example, if your blog is about beauty products and you know that there is a group of makeup artists and hairdressers in your area who meet regularly to give free demonstrations, tell them about your blog post.
If you are new to social media, this will greatly assist you and encourage you on this part of the journey.

Include images in your Tweets.
Use images to garner more attention. However, make sure that your image complements your content and it is a high-quality image.

Let us assume that you tweeted, "Guest blogger and Pastry Chef Molly shares tips on how to make chocolate croissants." With so many people tweeting, the topic may not be seen by your followers, or if they see it they may not be compelled to click on the link. However, if you have a photo showing delicious chocolate croissants, the imagery will cause people to click the link. They may not even read the entire headline, but the image is so appealing that they could not resist clicking on the link.

Make sure that the image you have chosen is not blurry. Also, check for background details. Regardless of which forum you are posting, this should not be overlooked. You may have a computer screensaver that says "I Hate Facebook," yet in your eagerness to show the chocolate croissants to the world you took a picture of them on a platter, forgetting that your computer screen is in the backdrop. Then you post on Facebook. Viewers looking at the picture will surely have lots to think and talk about, and it won't just be about the recipe for the croissants or how great they look. Their focus will be on what is on your computer screen.

Reserve the name you wish to use on various platforms.
You do not have to wait until you are ready to reserve a name. If you are still strategizing, you can sign up and save the name of your brand for future use. For example, if you are conceptualizing your website thebestfans.com, feel free to sign up for the "The Best Fans" on Twitter and Facebook and other popular platforms. That way if someone wants to steal your idea, you do not have to worry because you already own the name.

Moreover, though you may like a particular name, ensure that you conduct research first to determine if the name you have chosen is suitable for your business. You may be creative with a name but if the public has difficulty remembering the name or how to spell it, it may not be as creative as you think.

Schedule when you will check your accounts.
You have worked too much to simply ignore the feedback on the various platforms. You may wait with your phone in

your hand, or at your computer, assessing every comment, every like, every share, every reply to the comment, and check to see how many people saw your posts with the data that Facebook provides. That is time you could have spent working on your next strategy or writing your next blog post. Instead, set a time to check your posts. How often you wish to do so is entirely up to you.

Additionally, set your schedule so that you don't forget about your accounts. Do not post and then check back two weeks later.
Let you team promote your posts.
If you have a team, let them share your content. If you do not have a team, ask your friends and family to share your posts.

Share your content many times.
Sharing your content does not mean that you post your blog post, then share on Google Plus if you use that platform, then share on LinkedIn, then follow through with Facebook and Twitter. Share on every platform more than once. Plan a schedule.

Neither does this mean that you share on Facebook every 5 minutes. You can post on Facebook the next day or several days later. It depends on your traffic. If you have 2 people on your Facebook page, you will not have the need to post as frequently as if you have 200,000 followers.

Reply to individuals
If someone contacts you, try your best to respond in a timely manner. If you wrote about Easter discounts and someone asks a question, do not wait until it is summer to reply. By then you have already lost a customer.

Genuinely care about your readers and do all that you can to make their experience worthwhile.

Conclusion

Thank you again for downloading this book!

Content marketing is more than writing an awesome article. You have to strategize and take the time to analyze your data, observe social trends, monitor your social media platforms, and measure your performance. You have to assess what is working specifically for you and what is hindering your business growth.

Every platform that you use to distribute your content is not static. There are always dynamic changes. Whether it is blogging, using Facebook and Twitter, making videos, or emailing newsletters, you have to integrate the entire process to maximize your results.

Content marketing is not about you, but about your audience. Therefore, you have to adjust your marketing strategy because the behavior of people has changed. Consumers want information with more frequency than before, due to the advancement of technology. They want to gain more knowledge before they are influenced to buy, rather than have someone constantly imploring them to buy. Content marketing is about understanding the needs of your audience and helping them to make an informed decision.

I do hope that this book has offered a deeper insight on the steps you need to take to dominate your field.

Content Marketing

Strategies to Capture and Engage Your Audience, While Quickly Building an Authority

Introduction

I want to thank you and congratulate you for downloading this book, Content Marketing: Strategies to Capture and Engage Your Audience, While Quickly Building Authority.

This book contains proven steps and strategies for how to achieve a competitive edge and build your authority. I will reveal to you how you can use various components and resources and infuse them in your content marketing strategy. Once you apply them, you will attract more customers and they will become your loyal supporters.

Content Marketing involves knowing the dynamic relationship between your existing and potential customers' needs and the functionality of your product or service.

You must understand how your consumers view the world, how society, family, and their peers can influence their behavior, and how they realize their needs and desires. When members of your audience are motivated to fulfill their needs, they will purchase your product or service. However, you have to first engage them.

You will learn innovative and inspiring ways to capture anyone's attention. After implementing these strategies, you will connect better with your targeted audience, positively influence your audience's way of thinking, and obtain greater results.

Thanks again for downloading this book. I hope you enjoy it!

Chapter 1

Follow Your Passion and Popular Trends

Everyone has something he or she is enthused about. It can be sports, cooking, doing repairs, creating art, or taking pictures. When you complement your passion with other attributes such as discipline, patience, persistence, and a business mindset, you will be able to start a journey that will lead to success.

On this journey to success, there are some strategies you will have to implement to maximize your reward. You will have to market what you do in order to attract an audience. The audience will in turn purchase what you are providing and give you support because your passion not only gives you joy, but it provides value to their lives.

The type of marketing which we are focusing on is content marketing. Content marketing is using content to realize your business marketing goal. It includes PowerPoint presentations, newsletters, podcasts, videos, e-books, webinars, pages on your website, your social media channel, and blogs. Content is what you use to communicate with your audience.

What is your passion? What are your content marketing topics? If you are new in your respective field, perhaps you are examining potential topics. Whether you are already in business or you are just starting out, in order to become an authority in content marketing, it is essential to write on topics that you have a unique insight and are knowledgeable about.

For some individuals, this may be easy. For others, you may be unsure about what your passion is. Perhaps you have buried what you really want to do for so long, that now you are uncertain of whether you should pursue your aspirations. If other people around the world can do it, so can you.

Examples of People Who Followed Their Passion

Chicago native Brandon Stanton relocated to New York in 2010. He is a self-taught photographer who had resigned from his bond trading job. His goal was to take pictures of 10,000 people on the streets of New York. He started a photo blog entitled Humans of New York. The first year, it had hardly any reviews, but Brandon stuck with it and refused to quit. He is now successful, has published books, and has millions of followers on social media.

Jim Koch is a graduate from Harvard Business School and was a consultant with a Boston Consulting Company. He used his family recipe for Austrian Beer that had been handed down throughout the generations and produced Samuel Adams Boston Beer Company.

Classmates Jennifer Hyman and Jennifer Fleiss, who met while attending Harvard Business School, started Rent the Runway as they were enthusiastic about the fashion industry. The company provides more than 50,000 designer brand items of apparel for rent.

If all your bills were taken care of, you didn't have to worry about work, you had money at your disposal, and had a choice to engage in two enjoyable activities that can bring joy to the wider public, what would you select? What activities or skills you engage in, that your friends always compliment you about? Do not rush this process. Carefully take your time and reflect and then list the activities.

Once you have listed your topics, pick the one that you will feel more comfortable writing about. Realize that there are other people who will have the same passion, so choose the topic that regardless of the competition, you are confident of your capabilities as it is something that you are well-versed in.

The next phase is to fine-tune your topic. How can you make it even more innovative? For example, perhaps you are passionate about cooking. There are many blogs catering to this. What about your blog will be different? What type of cooking are you focusing on? French cuisine? Spanish dishes? Traditional cooking? Vegetarian cooking? Or are you one to experiment? Do you have secret recipes that your mother or grandmother passed on to you? After identifying your niche, consider what you will do differently to make you stand out.

Once you have selected the topic you will write about, you can create a blog. In the following section, I have provided a few examples of popular but unique blogs. If you are unsure about what topic to blog about, examine some of the popular ones listed below to help you get ideas. These blogs were started by people just like you. Their blogs are engaging and these bloggers are seen as authorities in their particular field.

Start a Unique Blog

Music blogs

Stereogum has over 57,000 subscribers. This blog focuses on indie and alternative music. The advantage of this blog is that it was one of the first on the market. Thus, they capitalized on it. If you are one of the few people blogging about a particular topic, your audience will definitely view you as an authority in your respective field.

This Song Is Sick is a blog dedicated to dance/electronic music and Pretty Much Amazing focuses on breaking music.

Entertainment blogs

Reality Tea is a blog that focuses on stars of reality television shows. Notice the uniqueness of the title, "Tea" instead of "Television."

Dread Central is a horror movie review blog. There are many horror movie fans and so the creators produced a very good niche.

Games

Sirlin Games is established by David Sirlin who is a game designer and player. He creates card and board games and sells them on his website and other websites.

The Farmville Freak Facebook page has over 400,000 followers. Though you may not be a fan of this game, you can focus on a particular game that you like and build your fan base.

Science

Universe Today focuses on astronomy. There are more than 69,000 subscribers. There is always a following when you share information about topics people want to know more about. This is definitely something different.

Humor

Garfield Minus Garfield is a very peculiar blog but it surely has its following. You know the cartoon Garfield? This is a blog that features Jon, the owner of the cat, without Garfield in it, hence the name Garfield Minus Garfield. So, if you are reading and viewing the cartoon, Jon appears delusional as in the original, he was talking to Garfield but on the blog he appears to be talking to himself. It has over 17,000 followers.

Graphics

PSD Tutsplus is a blog that focuses on Photoshop Tutorials. There are more than 165,000 subscribers.

Finance

Money Saving Mom is about providing information on how to budget and save.

Travel

Nomadic Matt is geared toward providing frugal travel tips when traveling. There are over 13,000 subscribers. If you enjoy traveling and you have much to offer to an audience, this is one way to share your wealth of knowledge with individuals around the world.

Sports

Arseblog is a blog totally dedicated to Arsenal Soccer. Are you a sports fan and know a lot about your team, more than the average person? This is one niche you can examine. However, strategize properly. Your blog should be seen as one of the authorities on your favored sport and team.

Do it yourself

The blog Makezine teaches an audience how to do certain things for themselves. If you have hands-on experience and wish to impart your skill, this type of niche may just be the one for you.

Language Learning

Fluent in 3 Months helps an audience learn a language in three months. If you know a foreign language, this is one way to develop a business and build your authority.

Exercise

YogaDork shares information about a particular form of exercise, gives the names of popular people who engage in it, and offers products to an audience. Rather than talk about exercise in general, perhaps you can focus on one area of it and build content around your particular preference.

Cooking

Smitten Kitchen is a personal cooking blog with over 200,000 subscribers. One of the unique selling points is that the kitchen is small. It is not a huge kitchen that is usually featured on those famous cooking shows. The bloggers identify with their audience and communicate quite distinctly that though you may not have the fanciest kitchen with the latest appliances, you can still cook a great meal.

Top 10 Lists

Listverse offers an audience the top ten for various topics. It's very informative and entertaining. If you are unsure of which direction you should take but want to blog, this can be an option.

Controversial Topics

DeSmogBlog was featured on Time's Best Blog in the year 2011. It was started in 2006 by Canadian James Hoogan. He addresses hot topics such as climate change and big corporations who make the problem even worse.

Beginner Tutorials

WPBeginner teaches WordPress beginners how to use the popular site. You can offer information for amateurs in your particular niche.

Art

Supersonic Art is an art and culture blog that features new artists.

How to know what is Trending

Use Keywords

Individuals seek people who can help them. They wouldn't ask a teenager to counsel them or ask a mechanic to fix their computers or ask the barber to apply make-up using the latest cosmetics on the market. Instead, they would seek a counsellor, therapist or psychologist, computer technician, and a make-up artist.

People look for sources to find solutions to their challenges and problems. One way in which you can build your authority is to be a resource for individuals looking to find a solution.

Today, everyone checks the search engines. The most visited website around the world is the Google search engine. Other popular search engines are Bing, Yahoo, and Ask.com.

To position your brand to be a source of knowledge for individuals around the world, you can use significant keywords, then write your content on that particular keyword. For example, if you sell skin care products, find the keywords related to your topic and produce the corresponding content.

One way to find keywords is by using Google Trends, which is an online tool designed for you to make comparisons of popular search terms. By using it, you will get a better understanding of the popular search trends. Just do a search for Google Trends and you will be directed to it. When you are on the page, type some key phrases into the search field and you will be shown a graph depicting the popularity of the word.

You can also search news headlines to survey what is popular in the news. If you are not a fan of Google, there are alternatives such as Bing Webmaster Tools and Majestic SEO. Enter the name Majestic SEO, for example, in your favorite search engine and you will be directed to the site.

When people are searching for particular topics that you have chosen to write about, they will be directed to your website.

Stay Up-to-Date on the Latest News and Research

Find a news source that is unbiased and authentic, and subscribe to gain information. That way, when a news report is published or there is breaking news in your particular niche, you can provide content on it. Make sure you give your own opinion. The objective is for you to be an authority, so write in your voice and style, using the news, research, or report as your supporting evidence.

Use Social Media

I will show you how you can use your various social media platforms to keep you informed about what is happening in your particular industry. In addition, you will learn the various methods on how to inform your audience about the hot topics so that they consider you as an influencer and an expert.

Chapter 2

Understand Your Audience

In order to create more appealing material and have an effective content marketing strategy, you need to have a deeper understanding on how and why your existing and potential customers act the way they do.

Abraham Maslow was an American psychologist who established what is known as the "Theory of Human Motivation." Maslow had six siblings and he was born and reared in Brooklyn, New York. His parents were Jewish immigrants who had left Russia to avoid persecution. Many people of his era had to cope with racism.

His theory is that there are vital human needs. He depicted it as a pyramid, which is commonly referred to as "Maslow's Hierarchy of Needs." At the base of the pyramid is what he refers to as physiological needs, and this includes food, water, clothing, sleep, and breathing. The next level above that is safety needs. This includes needs such as order, job security, and stability. When someone has shelter, food, and feels safe, they can achieve more in life.

Above safety on the pyramid is love and belonging. People desire to belong to a part of a group, have friends, be surrounded by family, and experience love. Above this is esteem, which is the desire of human beings to be respected, have confidence, have self-esteem, and have a level of success. At the top of the pyramid is self-actualization, which includes creativity, morality, the ability to solve problems, the acceptance of facts, and the lack of prejudice.

At the stage of self-actualization, people pay attention to themselves and build their image. This is where self-confidence and accomplishing goals are at the highest peak.

The levels below self-actualization are referred to as "deficit needs." This is so, as without those needs, individuals feel off-balance. As a result, they aspire to obtain them to feel contentment. One has to be mindful that an individual must have freedom to attain them.

The traits of people who are on the level to achieve self-actualization are:

☐ Highly creative

☐ They focus on solving problems

☐ Can view life objectively

☐ Pay attention to the well-being of humanity

☐ Have strong ethical values

The people who have attained the top level of the pyramid often:

☐ Have a strong work ethic and are responsible

☐ Engage in many new things rather than doing what everyone is doing

☐ They do not mind being unpopular

☐ They listen to their feelings

☐ They avoid pretense

These are just examples, and be mindful that no one is perfect. Though we all have flaws, everyone can achieve a level of self-actualization.

Based on what we have discussed, when creating your content, pay attention to your audience's needs. By using words that appeal to them more, you will capture their attention.

To help you engage your target audience more effectively, let us examine some other factors to take into consideration when creating your content.

Priming

Priming is the word used to describe when someone is exposed to a stimulus and it causes that person to respond in a particular way. For example, when you ask people to think of something that is blue, most people will say the sky or the sea. Or if you ask someone to name a fruit that is yellow, most people will say banana. How people associate things with color can be used in your marketing techniques and influence your consumers' behavior. You can use priming when designing your websites and when creating your content.

For example, if your blog is about meditation, you would not use a neon pink color for your website. If you have a romantic relationship blog, you would not use a gray background and dark images. Similarly, when you are wording your content, depending on your topic, you should use specific words and arrange them in your sentence in a particular manner to induce your desired feeling.

Do something nice

When someone does something nice for you, do you feel angry? Or do you feel special and have a warm feeling inside? Even if it is a person you do not know too well or it is a new place where you received your gift, don't you want to return to the place or stay in touch with the person? When someone goes out of his or her way and does something nice for you, don't you want to return the favor eventually?

When you are at a restaurant and the service is superb, do you compliment your waiter and leave a great tip? Do you return to the restaurant? If the service is very poor, on the other hand, you would think twice about giving away your hard-earned money. You may forget about dessert and hurry out of the restaurant when the meal is done, if you even decide to stay.

People usually do something nice for people who make them feel special. So rather than asking your audience to buy, buy, buy, give them something for free. Your audience will see you as someone who is sincere and helpful. You will be amazed at the results thereafter, when your target audience expands.

Peer comparison and conformity

Another strategy is using what is known as peer comparison, which is comparing someone to people of a similar group. For example, if I sell light bulbs, I may communicate, "Your neighbors use energy-saving bulbs to reduce their utility expense." By mentioning that your neighbors are doing it, will influence you to think that you should consider performing the same action.

Or if I sell phones, I may convey that X brand is better because it has more storage memory, a sleeker design, better functionality and business professionals prefer the brand. If you are in business, you would want to receive the best service and would consider upgrading as other people in your group, "business professionals," are using it. You wouldn't want to be left out. You would want to conform to what is expected of business professionals.

When you are providing an offer, use this strategy in your content. For example, if you have a PDF on your website for a free download, and you mention how many people in the same business niche have downloaded the book, it will pique a user's interest more than just communicating to your audience to download the book. Let them know what other people in a group are doing and saying.

Use scarcity

When there is an abundance of something, people are conditioned to wait longer to purchase it. Their mindset is that it will be available when they are ready. While preparing for a storm, many people would rush to get their groceries and other necessities when normally they would not. This is so because with everyone buying, there is no guarantee that what is needed will be available. Everyone at that point in time will be looking to fulfil their physiological and safety needs. The scarcer something is, the more it has value.

When wording your content, you can use this strategy, but be very mindful of how you word it. People tend to be more attentive when something is worded that there was plenty but because of the popularity of your service or product, only a few remain. If you communicate that you did not have a lot from the get go, it will get you traffic but not as much as if you let them know there were a lot of items, and so many people purchased them that only a few are left.

Pricing

If you are giving a discount, let the user know what the price was before, so they can be aware of the special deal they are receiving. You have likely visited websites where you have seen that something was priced at $19.99, for example, but a slash runs through it showing you that it is no longer that price. It is now $9.99.

Here are a few examples of companies who have applied some of these strategies.

We have discussed the ideology of peer comparison and conformity. Brand name clothing such as Givenchy send a message to the audience that buying the product will guarantee that they are in the exclusive group. Only fashion lovers with great taste will buy name brand clothing, and if you are not a part of the group, then your taste has to be questionable. It also relates to Maslow's 3rd level in that people need to feel loved and have a feeling that they are a part of a group. By expressing themselves by wearing certain clothing, people feel a part of the group. I am sure you have worn something you did not particularly like but you were told that it was fashionable and in style so you wore it, not to be viewed as old-fashioned and out of style. In wording your content, you would know how you can appeal to people's need for love and belonging.

When you think of Nike's slogan, "Just do it," it is very self-empowering. You can see the esteem need coming into effect with the words. People need self-esteem, confidence, and a feeling that they have achieved much. We all need that extra push and encouraging words. Why are you hesitant? Just do it.

You need to create content that satisfies the needs of your audience. For example, you may have a restaurant and your content focuses on the chef with his many awards, the ambience of your restaurant, and the abundance of great parking. However, one of the basic needs of people is food, not parking or knowing a great chef. If you have overlooked the food and neglected to convey that it is satisfying or use the necessary words that will appeal to the basic need for nourishment, then you have missed the mark.

Understand Your Audience

Be aware that you should not try to find a way to address the basic needs in every paragraph or everything that you write, but it is important to keep it in mind when crafting your content. Your content should make sense, not be absurd. When you look at automobile commercials, they usually address the safety issue. As much as a car may have a sleek design and a nice color, people want to know more about the safety features.

Consider skin care products. Most of them convey to users that they will feel and look younger. That is a great way to boost one's confidence.

How do you convey that your product or service will make your customers feel better about themselves? What value do you provide? Be mindful of the various needs in crafting your strategy, and give yourself time to be innovative.

Case Study

Tesla Motors was established in July 2003 and it designs, produces, and sells electric cars. The company was named after Nikola Tesla, the electric engineer and physicist. Tesla was born in Croatia 1896 and died in 1943. He traveled to other countries and worked with Thomas Edison.

The CEO of Tesla Motors is Elon Musk. He was born in South Africa and is the son of an electromechanical engineer. Elon later relocated to Canada to attend university and has degrees in physics and economics. He later moved to the United States and became a U.S citizen.

Elon expressed that one of the company's objectives is to offer cars at affordable prices for the average consumer. He established the Musk Foundation. Among other things, it provides solar-power energy systems where there is a disaster. In 2011, the foundation donated a quarter of a million dollars for a solar power project in a city in Japan that had experienced a tsunami.

Throughout the years, Tesla Motors has manufactured several cars. According to the company's 2015 annual report, there were approximately 13,058 employees.

Strategy

Tesla manufactures high-end cars, with wealthy buyers as the company's targeted audience. Then after a while, the company manufactured cars at lower prices for other consumers. Musk communicated on one of his blog posts, "New technology in any field takes a few versions to optimize before reaching the mass market and in this case it is competing with 150 years and trillions of dollars spent on gasoline cars."

Tesla has changed the way how things are done in the automotive industry. On March 31st 2016, Tesla displayed its all-electric luxury sedan known as Tesla Model 3. The delivery of the four-door compact sedan is slated for late 2017.

Seven days after the launch, there were reservations for approximately 325,000 cars. There were three times more reservations than when they had unveiled a previous model. As time progressed, more reservations were made on the Model 3.

Can you imagine that on the day the Model 3 was launched, thousands of people waited in line to make their deposit though they had not actually witnessed the launching of the sedan? Obviously, consumers know the quality of the brand and view the company as the authority and expert in the field.

Tesla competes with traditional car manufacturers. However, the company is the only electric car manufacturer on such a large scale.

Lessons

The company has been criticized harshly for targeting an audience that is wealthy and prosperous. However, from the beginning the company has communicated its vision quite clearly.

You have to be consistent with expounding your philosophy and your values. If you examine the company's content, the objective has always been to produce a low volume of cars to the affluent. Then the money will be used to manufacture more cars at a lower price and then invested again to create more cars at affordable prices for the average consumer.

The company wasn't secretive about its strategy. The company's objectives have always been available for anyone to read. The company's cars are so much in demand that people who are not rich, are willing to wait for the more affordable cars to be made.

Tesla finds ways to engage an audience. One doesn't have to dig deep to find information. As Tesla has constantly educated people on the changes in technology, people are changing their way of thinking. Over the years, they have been accustomed to how cars have been manufactured, but now they're willing to embrace a new way of doing things and purchase different car models.

Chapter 3

Quality Checklist

Have easy and clear instructions

On your website, examine where there may be areas where you can improve the experience for your user. If you have an app, the same thing applies. Do not have a framework that frustrates your users and make them think too much. There is a time and place for everything.

Social media is a forum for puzzles and it is entertaining. However, a user should not be puzzled trying to find buttons or the instructions on your website. Ensure that your website is built so that it is as self-explanatory as possible. A reader should be able to follow the instructions and know what to do next.

You cannot engage an audience until you first capture their attention. If the meat of your content is on the third slide show or page for example, how can your user navigate from instruction 1 and 2 to get to step 3? This is usually done when e-books or pdfs are given for free and you want the user to sign up to get to the next stage. Do not lose your audience between the various steps because the instructions are confusing. If so they will move on to another website.

Take the time to build your website properly and make the instructions easy to understand. Place it in an area where it is visible, also. Simple things like this can impair the confidence that people have in your brand or company. If you are making changes to your website, ensure that you follow the same procedure.

Easy scanning

Let us assume that you see a post on Facebook. You click on the link to read more about the article. After reading, you decide to quickly check other pages on the website. Do you scrutinize everything, read every article, and spend all your time on the webpage? Or do you quickly scan until you find something that is interesting? It is the same thing when individuals first visit your website—they will quickly scan until they find something of interest.

To assist your audience with easy scanning, use many headings so they can ascertain what the paragraph is about. Use short paragraphs so they can read quickly, and use keywords. Utilize bulleted lists and feel free to highlight key terms.

Have information quite visible

You may have a great website design, but if the information is hard to find, you will only lose customers. The information that people want to find without hassle include:

Opening hours

This is important especially if you are in the food industry. Imagine if you have a catering service or a restaurant, and after scrolling on every page, users still cannot find your hours. They will find another place to dine.

Telephone numbers

Ensure that phone numbers are easily seen and the information is correct. Have the correct format for your telephone number. You may have listed the information for people in your locale. However, what about people who may be calling from abroad? Did you include your area code? Is it convenient for an individual to have to research your area code to contact you?

Contact Us Form

If you are serious about engaging an audience, your form needs to be prominently displayed.

Do not ask for irrelevant and private details

You may have forms on your website for users to insert their information. Do your research and ensure that the information you have asked for is absolutely necessary. Asking users which company they work for and their pay grade is very intrusive. Ask information that is relevant and will not make your users skeptical about filing in the form.

Engage in testing

Whatever your line of business, if you have created something or if you have an app, ensure that you engage in proper testing. You may have designed it and you think it is the best design, but remember that you have the knowledge on how to navigate your way around it. Find someone and allow him to use it for the first time, to ascertain whether it will be confusing for him. Always engage in testing before you produce anything for the public.

For example, have you ever gone to the supermarket and you journey through the aisles and minutes later your shopping cart is still empty because you cannot find anything? After questioning the staff, they inform you that they rearranged the shelves. However, because you are accustomed to certain items being on certain aisles, you were lost. Do not take anything for granted. If you must change certain things on your website, alert your audience as to where they can be found. Before you launch anything, test it to make sure the desired results will be attained.

Do you have a strong strategy?

Perhaps you wrote your strategy in bulleted points, somewhere... if you can only find it. You have certain things in your memory, so you may decide to jump in and put everything together. It does not work like that. Every building, before it is built, has an architectural drawing. You must have your strategy on paper so that you can analyze and evaluate accordingly. Do not take this step lightly.

Added value

Perhaps by now you have a regular routine to post your content. Your editorial calendar is filled with dates and you have a steady stream of topics to write about. Remember, though, that it is not just about creating content but creating unique content. There are certain topics that everyone writes about. How can a user differentiate your topic from the next blogger's topic? You must invest time, plan carefully, and produce refreshing content. If you decide to cover topics that are trendy, write it from a different angle. Otherwise, your content will be lost amidst other related topics. One question to ask yourself as a measuring stick is this: What extra value do I provide to my audience?

As stated earlier, you should repurpose your content but try to avoid rehashing other people's uninteresting and dull topics. Thoroughly do your research. You will be surprised as to new information you may find so that you can inject zeal into your material.

Link quality websites

In my Content Marketing Beginner's Guide, this was highlighted:

An inbound link refers to a hyperlink that is on another site and leads back to you. An inbound link is sometimes called a backlink.

For example, if you are having an event, you will advertise it in your business place. You may also ask businesses to advertise your event and they may give out flyers to their customers. Individuals reading the flyer will know that you exist and will know more about your business. Using that analogy, if this was online, then the business will provide links to your website so people can click the link and be directed to your website.

When you have a lot of inbound links, search engines will rank your page higher on the list. Inbound links are referred to as off-page search engine optimization.

Note, however, that you should be aware of the sites to which your content is linked. Research properly and have a list of top quality websites you wish to focus on. Submitting your material on low-quality sites will not enable you to be an authority in your field. If hardly anyone is reading your work, and search engines do not register your site, your efforts will be in vain. Though you may like a website and wish it to feature your work, ensure that the site has a steady flow of traffic. Your goal is to build your audience.

Create content with your purpose in mind

Sometimes we get so excited about what we are doing that we lose track of our ultimate goal. Remember to focus on your content marketing objectives. You will have your own specific objective, but the purpose of this topic is to also capture and engage your audience to build your authority. Therefore, make sure the writing style you have opted to use for your audience will make them pay attention and have them wanting to read more of your content. Know your audience and write appropriately for them. Who are you writing to? Teenagers? Parents? People in the business field? Individuals wanting to know more about technology? Pet lovers? Is your writing style and the information you have given appealing to your audience?

After analyzing your data, has the profile of your audience changed drastically from when you initially started? For example, if your intention when you started your health blog was to cater to women, but you now have a growing male audience, have you factored in men's desires and interests in your articles, too? Or are you still mainly writing for women?

After you have produced your work, examine it and reword certain sentences or paragraphs if necessary.

Update your content regularly

After you have captured your audience, you have to constantly keep them engaged. To do so, you have to update your content regularly. You may have written on a particular topic one month ago and have received great reviews. Now that they know your topic inside out, what next? To be branded as an authority, you have to provide pertinent information quite regularly.

Hardly will you find that search engines rank websites that have outdated content. You can use evergreen content to rank consistently, but if your topic is about something for which your audience will need news updates, keep a steady stream of content to keep your readers interested and educated.

Utilize marketing platforms

Your content could be deserving of an award. However, if it is not strategically placed to capture new followers, your efforts will be in vain. Though you may use one platform in your personal life, in business you have to branch out and learn how to use other social media platforms as well.

Chapter 4

Expand Your Horizons

Be a Guest

Being a guest on someone's website or blog can improve your reputation and allow other individuals to see you as an authority.

Frequently make a valuable contribution to review sites, online magazines, and blogs, for example, to obtain new members. There are popular websites whose owners accept articles from guests. For example, if you are into technology, TechCrunch focuses on technology industry news and accepts guest articles. TechCrunch has over 6 million followers on Twitter and more than 2 million fans on Facebook. Forbes, which has been in existence since 1917, also accepts guest posts. There are some sites that may charge a small fee, but that is nothing compared to the number of subscribers your content will be exposed to.

Participate in Industry Events

Let us assume that there is a business seminar to be held in your area. Perhaps you may dismiss it for you have too much to do, like writing your content. However, as you brainstorm on how to capture new audience members, you may overlook that the business seminar is the perfect opportunity for you.

Select the events that cater to your type of business and participate in them. You will be able to bring brochures or other paraphernalia describing what you do. Attend conferences. Sign up to be an attendee, and if you also enjoy public speaking, sign up to be a speaker, too.

You have to position your material so that more people will be able to see it. Though online is an easy option, do not overlook the importance of conferences and seminars.

Sponsor Events

Let's assume that your brand is called Pet Corner and there is a dog show event that will be hosted in your neighborhood. You can sponsor it. Sponsorship does not mean you invest thousands of dollars and spend all your profits on an event. Be creative in the events you can sponsor.

If you are unsure as to the type of sponsorship you can be engaged in, let us examine this topic. First of all, sponsorship does not necessarily mean that you have to donate money. You can utilize "in-kind gifts," such as donating food in exchange for brand awareness. Moreover, you can be a promotional partner, which means that you can promote the dog show on your blog, for example, and in exchange, you get to speak to the public at the event.

Host Your Own Events

Rather than waiting to sponsor an event, you can host your own event. Your blog may have a great following, but you wish to capture a new audience. You can plan an event and ensure that is it memorable and entertaining to make an impact on your audience.

Be mindful that content marketing is a tool you use to achieve your business goals. Your goals should not be forgotten or neglected. It is not about producing content just to say you can produce it. It must complement your business goal.

By hosting an event, you can share your information in the way that you want to share it. When you attend an event, there is a structured way on how businesses have to conduct themselves and the time allotted for certain things, etc. However, when you host an event, you organize the best way to position your brand and material before an audience.

Remember it is not about you, it is about providing information to your audience. Continuing our example, you won't be speaking for 3 hours about how you started Pet Corner, and then name every dog you ever had and ask your entire family to share pet stories, and have slide presentations about your pets. Instead you should provide important information for your audience. You might have presentations on how to care for your pets, how often they should see a veterinarian. You might share information on the products pet owners may be interested in and have packages or brochures for them to take. Ultimately, you should share pertinent information that your audience will appreciate. You should have them loving your event so much they are looking forward to the next event.

An added feature is that journalists would cover your event. For example, if you have a cooking blog and host an event where you are teaching dads to cook so that they can surprise their families, it will make an interesting read in the newspapers and also via online news sources. By having journalists attend your event, you are showcasing to the public that you are an authority when it comes to your industry. You may not have the #1 cooking blog in the entire world, as there are giants such as The Food Network and famous authors with many restaurants, but you can own the #1 cooking blog in your area. Who knows? You may have such a huge following from strategizing and expanding your reach, that you may actually be able to have one of the famous chefs as a guest on your site.

Though events are entertaining, people attend them to be educated also. By hosting an event, you have an audience of people who are ready to learn. On social media, individuals' attention span is for a few seconds and there are also competing material that they have to sift through. With your own event, your audience is paying attention to you. Your rivals won't be there to showcase their information. People attended your event because they want more information from you, so capitalize on your opportunity. Show them why you are a leader in your industry.

Incorporate Cause Marketing

What is cause marketing? It is also referred to as cause-related marketing, and it is where a "for profit entity" and a "non-profit entity" cooperate for a charitable or social cause.

Case Study

Patagonia is an apparel company that was established in 1973. The company specializes in outdoor apparel and it is based in California. The founder of the company, Yvon Chouinard, is an American environmentalist and a rock climber. From 1985, the company's policy is to give 1% of sales to environmental associations.

One of their campaigns is known as the Common Threads Initiative and it was launched in 2005.

In 2011, Patagonia ran a campaign. There was an image of really cushy jacket. Just from looking at it, you can imagine how comfortable it would feel on your skin. However, the ad read, "Don't Buy This Jacket."

Huh? Why would a long-established company run an ad on Black Friday in the New York Times communicating to people not to buy the jacket?

Patagonia communicated to their consumers their message:

It's part of our mission to inspire and implement solutions to the environmental crisis. It would be hypocritical for us to work for environmental change without encouraging customers to think before they buy. To reduce environmental damage, we all have to reduce consumption as well as make products in more environmentally sensitive, less harmful ways.

Basically, the ad campaign was about bringing an awareness to consumers to be thoughtful when making purchases. The company did not want consumers to buy a product unless they really, really needed it. Furthermore, the company asked consumers to make a pledge. These are the salient points from the company.

Reduce

We make useful gear that lasts a long time

You don't buy what you don't need

Repair

We help you repair your Patagonia gear

You pledge to fix what's broken

Reuse

We help you find a home for Patagonia gear you no longer need

You sell or pass it on. (Ebay is a great place to start)

Recycle

We will take back your Patagonia gear that is worn out

You pledge to keep your stuff out of the landfill and incinerator

Reimagine

Together we reimagine a world where we take only what nature can replace.

What do you think about the campaign? Did you know about it back in 2011? If so, what were your initial thoughts? If it is the first time you are aware of it, what do you think? Does it seem complicated or is it simple to understand?

These are some of the comments

Comment 1

One individual said he promised not to buy the company's jacket.

Comment 2

Another individual was of the view that the company had encouraged consumers to be introspective and reflect on their purchasing habits. The company was commended for taking that initiative.

Comment 3

A guy commented that it was a "marketing ploy" and the company's message was not genuine.

Comment 4

A consumer was of the view that the company was being very "transparent" and if you do really need a jacket, there was nothing wrong with selecting one from Patagonia. The consumer further commented that it is better to support a company that is concerned about the environment and that acts in a responsible manner.

What was the outcome? Bloomberg featured the company in a 2013 article. It was revealed that there was a boost in sales by almost 1/3, so that the months of campaigning allowed Patagonia to net $543 million in sales in 2012. The next year their revenue was $575 million, which was a 6% increase.

Patagonia has made a remarkable impact on consumers. For individuals who are of the view that the company was not genuine, one must note that since 1985, the company has been involved in cause marketing. For many years, 1% of sales have been given to environmental associations. They have other similar initiatives.

Patagonia has always strived to be eco-friendly. In 1994, they used ecologic cotton after a company report in 1990 revealed that cotton was not good for the environment. The organic cotton demand boosted that particular industry in California. They are also involved in initiatives that help endangered species, protect animals, and address harmful human practices.

They have an Environmental Internships program where employees can volunteer for up to 8 weeks in a non-profit environmental organization and still obtain their full salary.

In keeping with their 2011 campaign, the company established a garment repair factory to repair customers' apparel.

Throughout the years, they have been consistent with their views and practices. They have attracted new customers. People who were not initial consumers supported them in the cause to have a better environment and eventually started purchasing their items.

The company also exemplifies how a business can personalize its message.

Let us compare Patagonia cause marketing with Coca-Cola's campaign.

Coca-Cola was established in 1886. Many years later, it was one of the leading global products. The company had a campaign in 2011 also, a cause marketing campaign that, unlike Patagonia, had many challenges.

The World Wildlife Fund (WWF) was established in 1961 and its objectives are to preserve wildlife and reduce harmful environmental practices. Coca-Cola teamed up with WWF to increase awareness of WWF's mission and to raise funds to protect polar bears.

The packaging to raise awareness was white cans with polar bears. Consumers were encouraged to give $1 donations online or by texting a code. Consumers mistook them for the silver can of Diet Coke. Many consumers, especially diabetics and weight conscious individuals, aired their grievances, emailed, and tweeted their anger and annoyance as they were confused.

There are reports that the company had planned to manufacture over 1 billion white cans but further production of the cans had to be stopped as consumers kept venting their frustration. Many people were confused by the packaging. The company then made the change of white polar bears on red cans.

The lesson is that you should be very cautious when changing or modifying an established image or brand. You do not want to confuse your audience.

Know your customers. Do not assume that a proposed change wouldn't really matter. Do proper testing, do research, have surveys and polls, ask questions, and analyze your data before you make bold and disruptive changes.

Pay attention to the visuals. The product was easily recognizable to consumers. There was a differentiation between the original Coke and the Diet Coke. The white polar bear on a white background totally blurred the distinction.

Coke has been in the business for over 100 years and so they had the resources to redo the packaging. Your business may not be able to withstand such negative reaction.

If you are using cause marketing as a strategy, be very cautious and ensure that research is done and proper planning is implemented. You want to build your authority, not damage your reputation or impair your customers' loyalty.

MasterCard used a rebranding exercise.

MasterCard was established in December 1966. Originally, the name was Interbank/Master Change. It is the creation of various California banks who wanted to compete with BankAmericard, which was issued by Bank of America. BankAmericard later became known as Visa.

The company's slogan is, "There are some things money can't buy. For everything else, there's MasterCard." The company has used the word "priceless" to promote the company's product and this tagline has been used since 1997.

For many years, the MasterCard logo has been a red circle and a yellow circle, overlapping in the center with red and yellow horizontal lines with the name MasterCard in the center. In 2016, after twenty years, the logo has been tweaked.

There are still the familiar overlapping red and yellow circles, but in the center, the horizontal lines have been removed and also the name MasterCard. In the center is the color orange and the word "mastercard" is place outside of the circles. The company kept the core colors to maintain people's level of trust and familiarity.

MasterCard Chief Marketing and Communications Officer Raja Rajamannar expressed in a July 2016 Forbes article:

First and foremost, we want people to know that our company is evolving. Evolving alongside them. The trust, convenience and security they have come to know when using MasterCard remains, and at the same time we are innovating and advancing for the future.

He was asked by the interviewer, Steve Olenski, what advice he had to share with marketers about rebranding. Rajamannar said:

This stuff is not easy. You've got to be really thoughtful about any rebranding. Firstly, resist the temptation to change the brand, for the sake of change. The equity and heritage your brand has built over time is an invaluable asset and you need to feel extremely responsible for it. A successful rebrand starts with a shared vision of who we are and what we stand for as a company, but the hard part is in finding the right expression that feels authentic and connected to our heritage, but also points to a vision for the future.

The new design needs to have qualities that will last for years to come, not something we'll just swap out again in five years. At Mastercard, we are rebranding after 20 years! We need to think about the look and feel of the brand and how it will sustain well into the future – it needs to have that staying power.

Thus, if you already have a product and you are thinking about rebranding it, you have to give much thought into what you are doing and consider the end results. Do not be too hasty to make any changes until you have looked at all your options.

Utilize Co-marketing

The more people who think like you and can work with you is very advantageous for your business. Both of you should have the same vision and be open to partnering in order to obtain mutual benefits.

Co-marketing is when two brands support and promote the other business service or product. The objective is to provide greater results in terms of reaching your audience and realizing sales. By teaming up, both business owners accomplish more than they could have imagined, as opposed to if they did it alone.

Note that co-marketing is not a joint venture. A joint venture is when two entities agree to start a business. That is not the only difference, another dissimilarity is time. Co-marketing plans are often structured for a shorter time period than joint ventures.

With joint ventures, at least one party must inject real capital to operate the business, and management is usually appointed by the joint venture. With co-marketing, both businesses contribute their own time, finances, and resources. Furthermore, their respective management arrangement is already in place.

The advantages of co-marketing are as follows:

Access to resources

Your brand partner may have access to resources that you do not have. This can include contact with industry influencers, software, or strategies. Be mindful of selecting brands that can offer you something that can capture a new audience.

Time-saving

Rather than having to spend several months to get access to a new audience or networking, by teaming up, the access is automatic. The time you would have spent crafting a strategy can be used to research and produce other awesome content.

Improves your reputation

You will expand your reach, and your brand will be more visible. The partnership will show the public that you are someone who can be trusted.

Exposure to new mailing lists

If both of you have a good mailing list, both brands can introduce each other to their audience. This will be new market for you.

Brainstorm and do your research and identify the list of brands you can team up with. Avoid having your rivals on your list of brands to approach. The key is that it should be mutually advantageous to both brands. The marketing effort should complement, not compete.

Identify businesses that have similar ideologies, persona profiles, but different services and products. For example, imagine you are a florist. You know of a business who is into event planning. It will be a perfect opportunity for your business and the event planning business to team up to showcase what you have to offer.

These are some other factors which you need to consider when selecting your co-marketing partner.

Assess the potential partner's social media profiles. Examine the type of engagement the business has with the audience. Assess the likes, followers, and the type of content that is being shared. Realize that your service or product will be marketed on the partner's social media, too, and so you should ensure that it is to your liking.

Are high-quality photos being used? Is the content engaging? When customers have queries, are their questions being answered? Look at the product or service reviews by customers. You may have a good perception about your potential partner, but what are the customers really saying?

Ask questions within your network. Ask friends and associates if they have any views about your prospective partner. When you do contact the person, ask appropriate questions to ensure that both of your goals are the same.

You are strategizing to build your authority, so do not team up with the wrong partner and impair your credibility in the process.

Pay-per-click (PPC)

Another tool used by businesses is employing PPC. How this works is that a business sponsors or buys a link which is shown as an ad in search engines. When key words pertaining to the service or product are searched in search engines, the ad appears.

We explored certain topics before, but to help you gain a better understanding, these things must be remembered. You can grow your website traffic by utilizing search engine optimization. Webpages and the content on your website pages are presented and ranked according to what the search engines find to be applicable. If someone looks for a specific topic in search engines, he or she will be given a list of information that is more relevant. The better your content, the more highly it will be ranked and noticed.

Advertising is a type of structured communication. With advertising, you are paying a third party to use their medium to capture an audience. For example, a business may pay a newspaper an advertising fee to showcase what is being offered. The business will capture the attention of the newspaper's readers.

Content marketing is about producing content to build your own audience. You can use social media, websites and even pay for advertising, as that is one channel to market your content. However, content marketing is about establishing your own audience. You can gain more mileage when you combine content marketing with advertising. One type of advertising is pay-per click.

When your ad appears and a user clicks on it, you will pay the third-party site or search engine a fee. You pay when the user clicks, hence the terminology pay per click.

For illustration purposes, let us say that you pay $2 for a click and when a user is directed to your website and reads your content, the end result is that they purchase $200 worth of goods. Compared to the $2 for the click, you have surely made a good profit.

When you create innovative and relevant pay-per-click campaigns, search engines usually charge less for the click. Google, for example charges less if your landing pages are helpful and satisfies the users.

You may wonder, "How can I ensure that I maximize this opportunity?" There is a resource called Google Adwords, which is the prevalent PPC advertising platform. You can produce ads to appear on the search engine and other Google resources.

Each time a search is done, Google looks at the advertisers and pulls the ads to be displayed in the ad space on the page with the search results. There are several factors that Google looks at while selecting who gets the ad space. The highest amount a business will pay and the quality score is taken into account by Google when making their assessment. The quality score looks at the click-through rate, the quality of the landing page, and relevance.

As highlighted previously, click-through rate (CTR) is the percentage of people that clicked on your link. The higher your click-through rates, the more it is seen as a success.

The frequency that your PPC ad is displayed is reliant on which keywords you selected.

Your PPC keywords should be appropriate. You have to allocate the right key words to obtain an increased PPC rate. Include popular terms that people search for and also the less common words. Once you have started your campaign, you have to monitor it to see if there are any changes you need to make.

It is always advisable to make the content and offer for PPC ads and landing pages suitable for your target audience. For example, perhaps one keyword phrase you use would be suitable for executives in big companies, and another keyword you use is suitable for smaller businesses. Therefore, you will create what is known as a split test for each group. This way you can analyze your data, assess which keyword is doing better, and make the changes where necessary.

There are various terms that are used for split testing which you may have come across. The term is sometimes referred to as 50/50 split test. It means that you subject half of a targeted audience to a test or landing page and the next half to a different version or landing page, and then make a comparison. The 10/10/80 split test is the same thing, just that you expose 10% to one thing, and the other 10% and 80% to a different version. A/B testing is another term used to mean the same thing. You divide your targeted audience into two groups, A and B, and observe which group performs better. For each PPC ad, conduct an A/B testing to see which target audience performs better.

For example, let us assume you are a life coach. You have written books on how to live a more positive life and how to focus on your future and not the past. These are ideas of terms which can be tested.

Your offer: Free counselling session versus Free e-book

Ad title: Self-help versus Seek help
Call to Action: Call right now versus Click this link
Reputation wording: Since 2008 versus Accredited
Price: $15 each versus 15% off

Once you have reviewed your data, you can determine which one works best. You will be able to ascertain which keywords are giving you the best conversion rates.

It is now time to go a step further. Are there parts of your geographical region where demand for your product or service is higher? If so, you can contact print publications, blogs, and websites that serve those regions so you can engage the audience in that area even more.

In addition, if there are locations where the response to your ad is low, strategize and formulate a plan on how to develop and promote your content to improve your brand awareness.

Chapter 5

How to be Prominent on Social Media

Twitter

Twitter was launched in 2006 and ten years later it is one of the dominant social media platforms. Users can send and view 140-character messages to millions of users around the world.

Over the ten-year span, the most retweeted image was a selfie that was taken by comedian Ellen DeGeneres with other celebrities at the 86th Academy Awards in 2014. She did it in honor of Meryl Streep's record nomination.

The other celebrities in the selfie with Ellen were Lupita Nyong'o and her brother, Angelina Jolie, Brad Pitt, Bradley

Cooper, Kevin Spacey, Julia Roberts, Meryl Streep, Channing Tatum, and Jennifer Lawrence.

Ellen tweeted it on her The Ellen Show Twitter page with the caption, "If only Bradley's arm was longer. Best photo ever. #oscars." When she posted it, it obtained more than a million retweets in the space of half an hour.

The record was previously held by Barack Obama in 2012 when he posted an image of him hugging the first lady and named it, "Four more years."

So how can you possibly capture your audience and maintain their attention? Let us examine some strategies to assist you. If you are new to Twitter or even if you have been using it for a while but have not been maximizing your fullest potential, you will learn new and exciting ways to share your content with your audience.

There were approximately 310 million active users by the first quarter of 2016. This does not include individuals who have accounts but check less frequently. So how do you get a slice of the pie of these active monthly users?

A term you should be familiar with is click-through rate, or CTR. It is the percentage of your audience that clicked on your link. It is the reaction to what you have posted at that point in time. The higher your click-through rates, the more it is seen as a success.

Ultimately, after you have implemented these strategies, you will determine which work best for you.

Interact with your audience's content

You already have so much work to do. You have to find topics for your content, update your blog, check your emails, check the comments, scan for criticisms from internet trolls, make sure all your links are working, check your editorial calendar and publishing schedule...and after that long list, you may raise your eyebrow when you look at this strategy. You may think, I don't have time to absorb myself in what other people are posting.

Interacting does not mean you spend 5 hours on Twitter. How long will it take you to like a post or to retweet it? Mere seconds. Look at it this way: it is a way to keep your brand in the spotlight. Twitter users will want to know who you are, what you do, and the service you provide. They will check your page. In addition, interacting with your audience's content can also greatly assist you in improving your relationship with your customers and potential customers.

Let us assume that you sell designer handbags. A customer tweets, "I want to get my friend a gift for her birthday. I need a cool surprise." You can simply like the comment. You did not tweet:

Buy one of my leather bags with the bead design. It only costs $49.95 now that I have a discount. Please visit the website www.leatherbeaddesigns.com.

You did not beg or grovel, you simply liked the post. Individuals viewing it will be curious as to who you are. They will go to your profile and website and see your stunning designs. By interacting with someone's post, you have captured an audience.

Retweet

Twitter users like when someone retweets their posts. It's a way of giving support and showing that you value them. Let's assume that you have a health blog. One of your customers announces that she lost 20 pounds. By showing your support, you can retweet it. Or if there is breaking news and you want your audience to be aware of something, retweet it so they can be informed. They will view you as a valuable source for information.

Moreover, by retweeting, all your support will pay off as your audience will also retweet your content.

Shorter Tweets are better

Twitter has a limit of 140 characters. Research shows that tweets with 80-110 characters and hashtags get shared more than longer tweets.

If a user wishes to share his opinion on what you have said, they will have space to add their own comment. On the other hand, if you use all 140 characters, an individual will have to modify your tweet so that he can add his view, and some people may think it too much of a hassle. Therefore, make it easier for individuals to add their opinions and also share your tweets with friends and followers.

Share links

Content marketing is not about keeping the spotlight on you and your brand all the time, every time. It is about sharing the value of your product or service with an audience.

Make sure that you insert links to your website and other pages you want your audience to visit. However, you must also share links that will add value to the lives of your audience. Of course, you won't send them to your competitors' blogs just for the sake of sharing. Share links that will make you and your business appear trustworthy and genuine.

Let us assume that you have a health blog. Perhaps there is a shocking report that a medical institution has just released. You can include it in your blog which you will update in the next two days as that is your weekly schedule. However, you can also tweet it with a link and further express that you will examine the impact of the report on your health blog.

Your readers will realize that you are sincere in your efforts to help people to be more health conscious. You didn't withhold the information—you shared it right away. By the time you update your blog, you will be surprised at the feedback as you have given your audience time to digest the information so that they can add more to the discussion.

Respond as best you can

Customer service plays a key role in content marketing. When someone tweets to you, do your best to respond. You won't be able to respond to every tweet, but you should respond to what you can, rather than ignoring them all.

When customers ask a question, or thank you for something you have done, reply so that they know you care about what they have to say.

Use Twitter Ads to increase your followers

If you have a budget allotted to advertising, you can pay for Twitter ads if you want more followers to engage in your content.

Use hashtags

Tweets with hashtags get retweeted more often. Therefore, try to have one in every tweet. By utilizing hashtags for topics that are trending, they will generate more traffic for your tweet.

Include images

You would know that 140 characters is really limiting when you have a lot to say. Try conveying your messages with pictures. Using the example with Ellen DeGeneres. Let suppose she said:

I am having a swell time with Lupita Nyong'o and her brother, Angelina Jolie, Brad Pitt, Bradley Cooper, Kevin Spacey, Julia Roberts, Meryl Streep, Channing Tatum and Jennifer Lawrence at the Academy Awards.

That alone is 175 characters with no spaces. She posted the picture instead and her wording was under 50 characters. To make your content more captivating, use images. It's also good to keep in mind that you can have several images in a tweet.

Post videos

You can upload videos from your phone with a time length of about 30 seconds. The attention span of internet users online is under 12 seconds, so the length of the video is appropriate.

Do not go overboard with your tweets

Having a schedule is important. When you have a schedule, you can determine when you will distribute information. This applies to Twitter as well. Be strategic. Do not tweet too much, as it will water down your content. Quality content is better than quantity. Big brands tweet about 1-3 times a day. When they post more than that, research shows that people interact less with the tweet.

Mention influencers in your industry

Mention popular people suitably and tag someone of influence to give your tweet more mileage.

Let us now explore how you can capture and engage your audience on Facebook.

Facebook

According to data from Statista, a statistic company, the number of people who signed into their Facebook account within 30 days for the first quarter of 2016 was 1.65 billion.

According to Facebook, 16 million local business pages were opened by May 2013. The previous year, there had been 8 million business pages. In the first month of 2016, there were approximately 50 million small business pages.

Observe the trends and align your content

Your audience and potential audience will constantly be talking about the latest trends. All you have to do is observe what is trending and associate your content with the hot topics. On Facebook, you can see what is trending by examining the newsfeed on the right sidebar.

Facebook has several methods of revealing what is shown in the news feed. The newsfeed is about delivering content to the right audience.

The top factors that increase what ranks in the newsfeed are:

☐ The user's interest in the creator of the post

☐ The performance of the post. For example, the likes, comments, and shares

☐ The performance of previous posts by the entity who produced it

☐ The type of post, whether it is a photo or status update, for example

☐ How recent the new post is

To have more people interacting with your post, make it personal. Be mindful that it is a business you are promoting so the personal information you share should be tasteful. Using the health blog example, let us assume that you have a staff of two and on your blog there is a health challenge to consume a restricted number of calories daily. You can post pictures of what you and the staff have opted to eat that day, along with the calorie intake.

Do not share your stories just on your blog. Share them on Facebook and other platforms. Let your stories be relatable, however. For example, you can talk about the ways you thought about cheating on your diet and the measures you implemented to ensure that you didn't cheat. Perhaps you removed all the temptations from your kitchen, like snacks and fatty food.

Your blog posts

Usually on your blog, there is an RSS feed which you should utilize. That way when you publish your post, it is automatically updated to Facebook. However, if you are posting a link to your blog by going to Facebook manually, make sure that you add a brief story or an excerpt so that your audience will know what it is about. Additionally, ensure that you have included an image that has the blog title attached.

Facebook will automatically use an image from your blog. However, let us assume that Facebook pulls your logo as that is the first image on your website, but instead you prefer the image of someone exercising, you can click the arrow on Facebook to see other picture selections—or just upload a photo directly on Facebook if it is easier.

Include videos

Don't just give a link to another page with the video, but upload videos to Facebook directly so that your audience can click and view them on that platform.

In August 2015, Facebook introduced live streaming. There was a restriction on who could use it. For example, it was limited to celebrities and journalists. In January 2016, it became available to iPhone users, and then in February it was available to Android users. Since March it is now available to all users.

For those who are unfamiliar with Facebook live, you should consider it to engage with your audience. It is available to every profile and page. The maximum amount of minutes your video can be streamed is 90 minutes.

To verify that your video is live, you will see a red icon at the top left and the word "Live" next to the red icon. You will also see the number of viewers.

After you have broadcasted it, it will be published to the page or profile and your audience who missed it can view it later. You can take down the video if you so desire.

Your audience can be notified when you post your video again. At the top of a live video, a user can tap the button that says "Live Subscribe." Thereafter, the user will be notified when there is a live feed again.

You should take advantage of this feature while it is new on the market. As most people are unaware of it, entertain your audience and use it to stamp your authority in your related field.

Not only do the videos show on your page, but also the newsfeed. On your page, you can utilize the customization and control settings when it has ended.

Inspire people

(This applies to all platforms)

We live in a tough world. Freedom of expression has caused some individuals to focus more on being negative and discouraging, rather than being uplifting. After a hard day's work, who doesn't want to be encouraged and feel inspired? We all do. One way to engage your audience is to inspire your audience by sharing motivational quotes. For example, if your blog is geared toward health, you can post quotes about being the best that you can be and don't quit. You can share great quotes from athletes to motivate your audience.

Use humor

Use tasteful humor to make your audience laugh. Do not use outlandish comedy and vulgarity, otherwise you stand the risk of offending many people.

Relatable posts

I'm sure you have seen those posts that make you remember your childhood. You do not even have to know who posted it, but you liked it because you can identify with the topic. For example, we all know the famous words that parents tell their children, "If you keep crying, I will give you something to cry about." If you are a parent, perhaps you have even used those same lines. Or how about this one, as a child you were punished in public and when you thought you could howl in protest and distort your face to show your anger, you were told, "You have 5 seconds to fix your face," or, "Fix your face or I will fix it for you." I am sure you remember when you questioned your parents' authority you were sometimes told, "Because I said so!"

These are just examples. Ensure that your relatable posts complement your messages and your audience will enjoy them. It is not about what you prefer, but what your audience will enjoy. You want them to like and share your posts, so post some really good content.

You can use word searches and puzzles

You can give puzzles and say to try and read the words upside down or have words scrambled in a box and communicate that the words the user sees is what he or she think about often. These are fun and entertaining puzzles that will have people sharing their opinions.

Math Quizzes

You can engage your audience with math quizzes for entertainment and educational purposes.

Have Contests

You can have your audience do a challenge and offer a reward. Using our example of a fitness blog, you can have an exercise challenge and offer free exercise gear, or whatever reward you want to give.

Share tips from the experts

What new tip or strategy have experts shared, but your audience may have missed it? You can share what was said. Perhaps on your blog you went into a long discussion. You can select an informative phrase or paragraph and post it on Facebook so your audience can digest it. Then you can provide the link to your website where they can read the full text.

Behind the scenes

Reality shows are viewed by many people around the world because they offer you the other side of someone's life. We all have our own daily battles to deal with. Sometimes rather than telling someone what to do, it has more impact when you also show them. Find a way to share behind-the-scenes moments with your audience. Be mindful that you should share something that will be valuable to them. It is not the time to air your grievances or shed the spotlight on you or your business.

Say, for example, that you are a life coach and your blog is dedicated to helping people transform their lives. Perhaps you went to a seminar and you blogged about it. You can share pictures of other attendees, for example.

They may see the post where you highlight what they need to do to make changes in their life, but let them see you in another light. Who helped you to make your transformation? A friend? A family member? A mentor? Do you care to share pictures of who the people are, once they consent? You can write about it and let your audience know how the individual has impacted your life. These are used as examples. For your specific niche, brainstorm and think of how you can implement this strategy.

Ask questions

You can ask questions. For example, where would you go if you were given a free ticket and time off from work? To assist you with getting more info about the profile of your audience, you can ask members of your audience questions. For example, using the life coach example, you can inquire, "Name one habit that you desire to change?"

From the feedback, you can get ideas about topics for your content. Let's suppose more people said procrastination was a habit they wish to change; you can provide information on this and guide them on how to make a positive change.

LinkedIn

Social network LinkedIn was launched in 2003. It is a professional platform. In the first quarter of 2016, there were over 400 million accounts, but 106 million accounts were active. Though it is based in the United States, it is available in 24 languages. In 2016, Microsoft has communicated that it will acquire LinkedIn.

There are various ways in which you can become an authority on LinkedIn, which we will examine.

Share articles from LinkedIn Influencers

On LinkedIn, you can find industry experts who share their opinions. Use this to your advantage. Research and discover specific articles from influencers on LinkedIn and share them in your network. Influencers can be known as they have a label on the right-hand side of their name. You may wonder why you should do this when you are struggling to find your own content. Why should you promote other people? Think about it. They are already the movers and shakers in their industry. When they communicate, people listen. On the other hand, you have absolutely nothing to lose and everything to gain. By providing something of value to your network, your audience will look forward to what you share and post. In this way, you are capturing an audience by using great info, and in time you will see your audience expand.

Moreover, your network more than likely will come across the Influencer's post. After all, they are influential people. You can benefit if you share the information first, before other people have gotten a chance to read it.

Share posts appropriately. Do not clog your audience timelines by you sharing many articles. They will see it as annoying. Know how often you will share articles.

Follow Influencers

Follow people in your field and also experts in other positions to inspire you. It will give you ideas on how you can be creative in your business, and on how to word your content.

Review Your News

In the "Your News" tab, you can view posts from the people you are following. Select 2 or 3 topics to read daily to obtain ideas. Be mindful that you have your content to draft, refine, post, and distribute. Allot a particular amount of time so you do not spend most of the day on the site when you have other things to do also.

Like and Comment

As you go through the newsfeed, do not forget to like other's people articles and feel free to comment. When you like and comment, you are paving the way for other people to notice you and follow you.

Join Groups

Select suitable groups and become a part of them. If you have joined a group and it is not advantageous for you, leave and find another suitable one. Join groups in your area if you are unsure about other groups. You can have more authority in smaller groups than when you have joined a group with 100 experts.

Additionally, ask questions in the group, conduct polls, and respond to other members' posts.

Instagram

Instagram is a video and mobile sharing social platform and it was launched in 2010. It was acquired by Facebook in 2012. By 2014, they had obtained more than 300 million users. Anyone can connect their account to Facebook and Twitter, also.

Using the Instagram Website

Note that the app is more used to post, while the website does not allow you to post. However, you can edit your profile, follow others, and search using the website. Visit Instagram.com from a web browser. Log in with your user name or password.

Using Instagram from your Mobile

You can use it from your website browser or your mobile. On your mobile you can download the app from the iTunes App Store or Google Play. If you're a user or if you're a beginner and have no idea what to do, I will give you strategies to engage and build your audience.

Download the app and sign up by entering your email address, select next, and log in with your Facebook account, if you have one.

Set up your profile picture and include information about your business. You can also link it to your website. Find users to follow by going to the profile tab and in the options settings, click Find Friends.

Post your video or photo by clicking on the camera icon on your app that is in the center of the bottom menu. You can record a video or take a photo or select one from your picture gallery. After selecting your video or picture, tap Next. Thereafter, you can utilize the filters and modify your photo by cropping or changing the exposure, for example. With your videos, you can change the length of the video or select the sounds you want.

The step after making your changes is to select Next where you can add tags or captions, location, and other social information. The last step is to choose Share.

Link with other social media accounts

You can connect your other social accounts so individuals can find you on other platforms. On the profile tab, go to linked accounts, then share settings. Choose the accounts you wish to link.

When you upload a photo, you can also decide which ones to share to your other social networks.

Hashtags

Add hashtags (#) to obtain new followers. Make sure you use suitable hashtags. When you type your hashtag, Instagram will provide you with similar hashtags so you can get an idea as to the number of posts.

Getting featured

Instagram selects users and adds them to a list. If you get added, there is a lot of exposure for you to gain new followers. To get noticed by Instagram, be consistent in the type of pictures you post, and have a distinguishable niche or style.

Add accounts

One feature that many Instagram users are happy about is that since February 2016, you can manage up to five accounts. To add an extra account, go to your profile settings page and select the image of the gear that is situated in the upper corner. Scroll and select Add Account. Open your account with another user name and password. To navigate between the two accounts, on the profile page choose your username and select the account you want from the pull-down menu. To remind you of which account you are currently using, you can simply look at your profile picture.

Conclusion

I hope this book has provided you with a deeper insight on how you can integrate various communicative tools and many other resources to achieve your business goals.

Researching the market and analyzing your data are very important when formulating your strategy. These components assist you in identifying the needs of your audience, creating new products and services, examining the effectiveness of your activities, and making the necessary changes. Testing is also a key component. It ensures that the level of your audience trust is either maintained or increased. In addition, testing allows you to correct any errors and strengthen any areas that may be substandard.

Furthermore, consider the social media platforms which you will utilize. Media planning is more than identifying which platforms you will use. You have to also determine when you will market your content and how often you will post your content. Each platform has its own set of variables that work best for businesses wanting to reach more users, so you should explore all your options.

Sponsorship is one way to acquire more interest in your product or service. You can either support an existing event or activity, or you can create your own. Interact more and network with other people. You can team up with another business to give your product or service more mileage.

Get involved with what members of your audience are doing. Follow them on social media and support the positive things that they engage in. Let them realize that you are genuinely concerned. Join groups where appropriate, ask questions, and take polls to get a better understanding of how you can better serve your audience. The people you support can one day be your most valued customers.

Content marketing will take time, but once you plan properly, treat your audience respectfully, and apply these strategies, you will achieve your business goals.

Content Marketing

Tips + Tricks to Increase Credibility

Introduction

This book contains proven steps that will guarantee that your brand appeals to a wider audience.

The method of marketing has changed, and so should your approach. You have to review your overall framework and make the adjustments where necessary. Your content should be a reflection of your brand and your voice, harmonized with your customers' needs and desires.

Once you implement what I have revealed, you will improve your credibility with your colleagues and your audience. Content marketing is much more affordable than the traditional methods of marketing, and very effective once done correctly and with supportive structures in place.

You will need to dedicate the time to improve your skills, and if you have staff members, their skills as well. You will need to work on your business strategy and distribute your content on various platforms. You will receive higher returns, more commendations, and a continuous flow of revenue once you apply these successful tips and tricks.

Thanks again for downloading this book. I hope you enjoy it!

Chapter 1

Website Framework

Your website is more than an online structure to display your content. You have to pay attention to the appearance of your website, the ease of access to your content, and the usability.

Your website represents your brand and your staff. Your website must complement your goal and have a good impact on your viewers. You will have to update your website continuously.

Technology has changed the appearance of websites. A responsive website design (RWD) automatically allows for your website to adjust according to the device a viewer is using. On the other hand, if your design was before this development, you will have to make sure that the mobile and desktop versions of your website have the appropriate settings and the appearance is suitable for viewing.

When someone visits your website, will the viewer be confused or will they be able to navigate easily? Does your website allow the viewer to comprehend the value of your product or service? Will viewers know the advantages of using your product or service? Does your website have a big image of the product and the Buy Now button without having a product description? Have you given sufficient information about your product?

Your website is available to your audience around the clock, thus making it convenient for anyone to contact you. Customers do not have to wait until your store opens or until the day begins to air their grievances or concerns or give great reviews. They can simply send an email or fill out the contact form or comment on certain pages, anytime and from any location.

Your website allows you to continuously serve your existing customers and give potential customers information that will guide them in making purchases.

The more professional the presentation of your website, the more advantageous it is to you. Here are certain features that you should ensure are presented professionally and skillfully in order to enhance your brand and reputation.

Contact Information

Having your "Contact Information" signals that you are someone who can be trusted. This is extremely important as today anyone can have a website and use fake names to mask his or her identity. People want to know who they are interacting with.

Your contact information is an indicator of how open you are for scrutiny. If someone is going to take what you say to add value in their lives, they should know exactly who they are getting the information from. Refraining from sharing this essential information and only opting for people to contact you through a form can be a bit impersonal. There is nothing wrong with having a form, but if your reader does not know where in the world you are located, you leave them to wonder. They would be curious as to who is behind the company. Whether it is someone who can be trusted, or if there is something to hide. If your audience has an issue or challenge that needs to be resolved quickly, who should they contact? How soon will the contact form be checked, and when will the individual receive a response?

Sharing an email address and a physical location, or including a phone number if you do opt to do so, will eliminate the concerns that a person may have.

You do not necessarily have to add the contact information on the Contact Us page. You can add your phone number or have a link to your email in the header of each webpage. If you are a large company, you can have "Contact Us" on the top navigation rather than having it in the footer of your webpage.

Be mindful that it is not everyone who will be surfing your website or blog on a desktop computer. For mobile users, it can be challenging to find the "Contact Us" when it is deeply buried in the footer amidst other links you may have.

About Us Pages

Have you ever read a business About Us page and you wonder if you had ever surfed that website before as the text sounds so familiar? Most likely you have not been on it before, but the text sounds so familiar because it is the standard information that everyone uses. Same mundane text, same wording, same format. The content may sound engaging and humorous, but there is a detachment with the About Us page.

What about your company is unique and different from your competitors' companies? Why not use photos? Or use a timeline? The photos do not necessarily have to be colored. They can be black and white if it enhances your business. For example, if you are selling artefacts or art, perhaps black and white pictures can be more appealing to an audience.

Do not use immaterial pictures. Imagine you have an About Us page and you are sharing your story about being a fashion designer and how you started when you were a teenager. However, on the About Us page, you use a picture of the building you are based. All a viewer sees is blue skies, a concrete building, and the sidewalk. The viewer would have preferred to see what is happening inside of the building. Who is inside the building? Ensure that your picture complements the information you are conveying.

Bios

If you are giving bios of the various team members or employees, ensure that they are thorough and the pictures are presentable. Imagine, for example, that you are in the business of counseling. Your content reads so well that your audience is ready to open up and share with you their fears and concerns. You have really connected with your audience. Then they open the page that showcases the bios and there is a picture that startles them.

A picture of one of the workers was taken when he or she was unaware. The worker was upset about something when the photographer snapped the picture. Frankly, the picture looks very mean. When the website was ready to be launched, the worker was absent and so to fill the gap, the mean-looking image was used. Who wants to be vulnerable and share intimate details of their life with a mean-looking counselor? In reality, the person may be the sweetest and gentlest employee, but the viewer would not know that. A very important detail has caused you to lose your credibility.

Another point to note is that a sparseness of information can also lower your credibility. For example, on the bio page there may be pictures of workers and names, but what do they do exactly? Who works in the sales department? Who is the manager? Who are these people? They can be random pictures pulled from the internet. Do not leave any room for your viewer to doubt the authenticity of what you have revealed.

On the About Us page, you can also include videos, any notable awards received, community or charitable events, and testimonials.

Provide Names of Previous Clients

Make sure that you are not breaching any agreements, and once it is okay, you can name some of the clients you worked for. Using our previous example, if you offer counseling services and a viewer realized that you worked with X Institution and Y Institution who are reputable companies, it will improve your rating. Especially if X and Y Institutions are highly regarded in their respective business arenas.

Do what works best for you. You can give the names of clients on a specific page, or include the names on part of a page such as the home page, or you can use their logos if you prefer.

Uniform Logos

Do you have a logo? Is it the same logo that you have used on other platforms? Imagine, for example, that your logo is a sun with red shades on it. You have promoted it on your Facebook page, your Twitter page, and other platforms with the link to log on to your website. Readers click the link and instead there is a picture of a star and the moon as your logo. What happened to the sun and red sunglasses? Even if you have changed it, make sure your logo is uniform across all platforms, otherwise you will confuse readers.

If you do not have a logo and use an image, the same rule applies. If your blog Pet Corner has a picture of pets, do not use pictures of cars on other platforms. Make sure that you develop your brand and improve your brand loyalty as opposed to doing certain things that make your audience view you questionably. By having different pictures or logos, you are indicating that you are unsure of what you are doing. People cannot trust someone who is uncertain about what they are doing.

Design and Colors

Do not publicize your website until you are absolutely sure that it is the final product. Choose your themes and colors carefully. Also be certain about the layout you would like to use. Imagine that your blog, Pet Corner, uses a cream backdrop with a side panel showcasing your various content. Your readership has grown and people like the simple design as they can navigate their way around it much better than others.

One day, you visit your competitor's website. The competitor seems to be doing well and instead of focusing on your business objectives, you decide to follow exactly what that person does. You change your cream backdrop to a bold red and put the articles at the top instead. Your readers log on and the color red dazzles some of your readers' eyes so much, that they cannot stay long on the page.

The other supporters that try and bear with the loud color then have to learn their way around the website again. It so happens that in your attempt to change the website, you forgot your mobile users. For those checking on their mobile devices, everything looks confusing. You did not test to see how it would look on a mobile device. Therefore, it becomes one big frustrating experience and they go somewhere else to see adorable pictures of pets.

There is nothing wrong with changing your website after you have launched it, but ensure that the changes are more beneficial for your audience. Also, be mindful of your mobile users.

Be Transparent

If you have e-commerce on your website, make sure that you are transparent throughout every step of the purchasing process. Keep your audience informed about the status of the product and when it is expected to be delivered, if delivery is involved.

When someone uses a card, make sure that the invoice reflects the price. Can you imagine how you would feel if you bought something for $5.99 on a website and the invoice shows that $15.99 was deducted? What if you were told, after your query, that the product is really $15.99 but the 1 was missing in front of the 5? Or what if every month your card is billed $15.99 when you only opted to purchase it once and not every month?

One bad experience like that can be detrimental to your business. Therefore, do not defraud your audience. If they had a good experience shopping with you, most likely they will return, and also tell others about you.

Choose Images Carefully

Let your images appropriately reflect the content. For example, if you are sharing a story about a vacation abroad and a product that will help your audience, a picture of the landscape may look beautiful but it will have more impact if you include a picture of the product.

Or if you are communicating about your recent trip abroad and your only pictures are of the airport in the area where you reside with you holding your suitcase, it will have less impact than if you actually shared pictures of your trip.

Testimonial Pages

What better way to increase your credibility than to have satisfied customers market your business for you? How can you do this? Create a Testimonial Page where they can feature their great experiences.

Blog

You can have a blog to update users about the business or have engaging discussions. Remember that the blog, like your other sources, is to provide information that is worthy to your reader.

Chapter 2

Your Content

Refrain from acting like a salesperson

Are you annoyed when a marketer calls you over the phone? You wonder how they obtained your number. Politely, you inform the person you are not interested in what they have to offer. You sigh in relief as you hang up. Then 24 hours later, the person calls you again. You politely explain that he may have misunderstood you, but you are not interested in his product now or in the near future. The following day he calls and informs you that he has a new product that you may be interested in.

No one likes to be harassed by salespeople, so do not do the same thing with your content. You can word your content in such a manner that though you have various products and services to offer, the viewer reads it as information and not an annoying sales pitch.

Your focus should be on the reader and not on your business product or service.

Educate your supervisors and staff

If you are working in a company and have to provide content, you may need to inform your bosses about content marketing. They may at times pressure you to include more information about the company's product and service. However, as highlighted in the previous point, you should not sound like a showy salesperson.

Content marketing is about obtaining readership with the hope that in the future, it will cause your audience to purchase and support your business. Bosses at times may just see the end result, not understanding the process that will take it there. They may not understand the difference with content marketing and advertising.

Advertising is structured and is one type of communication. Advertising is usually prejudiced in favor of the advertiser and brand, and there is a line of distinction between an advertiser giving a point of view and on the other hand misleading the public and producing false expectations.

With content marketing, you are providing information with the audience as your focus. Your brand should not be the main focus. Some people may not understand the difference so you may need to shed some light.

Likewise, if you are hiring people to write your content, educate them on the differences as well, if they are unaware.

Wear your reporter cap

Refrain from being an aggressive advertiser and start being a reporter. You do not have to be on television or on radio to start thinking like a reporter. What I mean is that you should produce material that really informs your readership.

Reporters usually give details—the how, the why, and the when factors come into effect. What details are you providing in your content?

Check over your facts

You have toiled long and hard in researching your information but one minor detail that you may have mixed up or omitted can damage your credibility. If you had hoped to publish your content by 3 p.m. on a particular day, but you need one hour to check it over, do so. One hour delaying your publishing time is better than saying that 90% of X does something when in reality you meant to type 19%. Sometimes writing while tired can cause anyone to make more errors than normal, so re-examine what you have written before sending it out to the world.

You can have someone read over your work if you are not good at spotting errors for yourself.

Additionally, if you used a source, you can provide a link to the original source. For example, if you are saying that Dr. X of Y Institution in a report stated that something is beneficial, you can provide the link to the actual report. It is not like you are providing a link to your competitor's website, so what do you have to lose?

People are more likely to trust material that has supporting information, especially when it has named sources. For example, rather than saying a doctor said something is beneficial, you can name the doctor.

Even if the source just happens to be an uncle or parent, mention it, as it reads better. Rather than saying, an individual once told me that one of the secrets of living a happier life is..., tell them who that individual is. Readers will want to know who gave you the information and what makes him or her such an expert? They may wonder, is this individual referring to a 19-year-old? A 19-year-old hasn't even started to figure out life as yet, so even though that might not be the individual you are referencing, your readers have been left to wonder.

On the other hand, if you write: My 75-year-old father once told me that one of the secrets of living happier life is..., that has more weight than leaving your readers in the dark. Advice from someone in his seventies is definitely worth listening to. Name or describe your sources. Writing a 75-year-old is good, but actually informing the readers that it is your father has only added a more personable touch. You have opted to share a private moment and advice with the rest of the world.

Do not go overboard, of course, as the material is for your audience so you won't talk about irrelevant information and use it as if the spotlight is on your family, when the spotlight should be on your readers. Be wise enough to know when to give private details.

Share your work

This is basic. You are probably thinking Facebook tabs, Twitter links, and other social media platforms. This is extremely important. However, while you are busy sharing with people you do not know from all parts of the world, you may have neglected those who you do know and will welcome the information, too.

Do not forget to share your work with friends and family. If your friends share your work and someone asks who wrote it, and the answer is, "My friend from college," it has more weight than saying, "I have no idea, I just saw it online."

Listen and read the comments

As your readership grows, keep more in tune with what others are saying about your content. The key word is "more." Even if you have 5 followers, they are just as valuable as if you had 5,000, so listen to what they have to say. As your readership grows, you will have more comments, and by the same token you should read them and check them more often.

By keeping tabs on what comments are made, you will ensure that your content is not misinterpreted or taken out of context. This can impair your credibility, so once you spot something you can inform the individual or individuals that that was not what you meant.

Additionally, by checking your comments, it gives you a better understanding of who your readers are. For example, if you notice that every time you provide information on a particular topic, many people with religious views attack what you wrote, then you have a better understanding that your readership is more religiously diverse than you realized. Perhaps you need to elaborate more or write with more clarity or simply delete the comments if it appears that your attackers are internet trolls.

Internet trolls

"Internet trolls" or "trolls" are individuals whose objective is to harass and tear apart what a writer has written. They are not genuinely concerned about having constructive criticism, but disrupt forums and try to lessen the significance of your material. For example, your readers may have contributed "Great article" or "I learn a lot thanks." Even 400 people can comment that the content was informative and has helped them tremendously. The internet trolls may say, "Yawn. Boring!!! This article has no substance. It's a waste of people's time. Were you depressed when you wrote it?"

Internet trolls are everywhere, and at times you can ignore them. If 400 people commending an article and just 1 person is rude and obnoxious, it's worth ignoring that 1 person.

However, if you have provided facts and the internet troll says, "You're wrong, the report says it was 25% and not 40% which you wrote," it is best to comment and provide supporting information if you had not already done so in the body of your content. Let's assume that you failed to provide links for your readers to verify what you have said, and you also ignored the comments; the comment by the troll can negatively impact your credibility. You have to keep abreast of what people are saying. If you do not wish to check the comments, you can assign someone you trust to check for you.

Include powerful words

Use strong and influential words in your content. Rather than saying, "We have good news to share with you," you can write, "We have splendid/awesome/tremendous/amazing/ remarkable news to share with you." You can use either the word splendid, awesome, or tremendous, and the list goes on.

Speaking with your peers is one thing, but communicating with the wider world is a totally different ball game. Remember the end result is that you would like your readership to purchase your product or service eventually. You have to attract them and offer your best. Your friends know you and have a soft spot for you, so saying "good" news to them would not make them adore you any less. Your readers, on the other hand, have no idea about you other than what you have shared in the About Us page, so your words should be very compelling.

Add some better adjectives to your content. Make sure you use them appropriately, though. In your zeal to convince, do not say, "Splendidly, we wonderfully and awesomely have some remarkably and tremendous news to amazingly share with you." It sounds absurd and shows that you are trying too hard.

It is always best to hire someone who is experienced rather than have content that is all puffed up and sounds awkward.

Reveal almost everything in the opening paragraphs

Once ago, people had the time to sit and surf the web while drinking coffee or their herbal teas. Life moved at a slower pace. People had time to scroll and read and read some more. Though the content may have been a bit challenging to sift through, they would read to the end, finding the value in what the writer conveyed, even if the main point was placed at the end of the article.

Today, there is so much information to digest. People walk and scroll and run with coffees in hand, and click while running. They move along if the headline is dull. The behaviors of internet users have changed since the mobile revolution. There are so many apps, so may social media platforms, so much stuff. How do you possibly obtain their attention?

People do not wait until they get to the end or scroll and scroll to find the value like once before. You have to grab their attention from the beginning. The attention span of readers is under 12 seconds. Therefore, your headline has to be engaging in that span. Once you have appealed to users, maintain that level of attention. Do not throw away that opportunity. They saw your headline in those few precious seconds and they clicked on it with anticipation, so continue to hold their attention. Your opening paragraphs should reveal almost all of the important stuff. Convey what you wish rather than saving it at the end. Once you have given them almost everything, get them to read to further along and then you can reveal the rest.

Use more visuals

Referring to what was said above, people's attention span is shorter than it was years ago. It helps to include more visuals where you can. For example, if your blog is called Pet Corner, rather than typing one long paragraph on social media about this cute image you took the other day of your dog and the neighbor's kitten, show the picture. Who doesn't want to see an adorable picture? Even if the reader may not be a pet lover, if the picture is really appealing, who can resist clicking on it and being led to your blog post?

Ensure that your visuals are of high quality. Fuzzy pictures and out of focus pictures do not leave a good impression. Therefore, check the quality of your images.

Describe the value of your content to your audience

Customers want value. Help them to understand the value that you offer rather than leaving them to figure it out. Do not use your content as if it is a puzzle, giving clues and making readers find the answer. Rather than a 500 to 1000-

word article on how your product or service will help them, tell them from the beginning.

A business may want to offer a graphic course for beginners. Look at the difference at how it is communicated.

1. Sign up now for my graphics course.
2. Learn the secrets and advance your career as a graphic artist by signing up now!!

Surely, the second example is more compelling than the first. Who doesn't want to learn the secrets to developing one's career? That's great value for a beginner. Even someone who is not a graphic artist may be persuaded to sign up just to learn something new.

In your business, what value can you provide to your audience? What are some of the ways you can describe it? Be creative and do not be reluctant to reach out to those who are experts in the writing field.

Refrain from being unclear

Here are two examples
1. Learn how I lost a lot of weight over a period of time.

2. Learn how I lost 250 pounds in 5 weeks.

The second example is packed with information that people can trust. You specifically said how much was lost and how long it took you to lose it.

The first example is very vague. What if someone clicks on the link with high hopes that perhaps he or she has found the solution, and when they read the information, they discover that you lost 2 pounds in 4 days? Or that it took you 5 years to lose 10 pounds? Anything you post after that with your vague headlines will be completely ignored. Being precise is an essential element in gaining someone's trust.

Moreover, vague information in the body of your article is just as damaging. Let us assume that many people clicked on the headline: Learn how I lost 250 pounds in 5 weeks.

In the article, you talk about a trip you made to India and you discovered some herbal teas. You drank one specific type in the morning and the next type before going to bed. You absolutely love the teas as they changed your life. You then encourage your readers to drink more herbal teas. Then you end the article with a picture of you smiling in India.

The reader then scrolls back up, and scroll down again. They may even turn off their device and turn it back on, thinking that the internet connection perhaps was slow and it failed to load an image or video about the name of the tea. The person may reread the content, searching for the answer, only to realize that you were so concerned about telling them about your life, you failed to mention how you can add value to their lives. You didn't mention the name of the tea or where your readers can obtain it.

Remember the content is not about you. Save the vagueness for strangers who will have no impact on your business. By being vague, you will drive your audience to other websites that give information.

Use questions

Using questions in your headlines makes your readers more curious. It makes the content more conversational.

1. The story of Facebook
2. Do you really know who owns Facebook?

The second example causes the reader to pause. He or she may wonder if they missed the news and that it has changed ownership. They will click for more information. The first one, The story of Facebook, sounds less interesting.

Simplify your content

You are not writing to impress your bosses. You have not applied for the role of English lecturer at a university so there is no need to use language that would intimidate even a college student. Your vocabulary may be extensive, but it is not about showing how smart you are. It is about ensuring that your audience understands your message. Refrain from using complicated language and examples that leave your readers more confused.

Shorten your paragraphs

Write as if your audience is in junior high if you have a tendency to go overboard with the length of your paragraphs. Keep paragraphs short and have a clear message. Do you remember those days in school when teachers asked you to read the text and then quizzed you on what you read? Sometimes you had no idea what to say because you hadn't understood it in the first place. Do not leave your audience feeling confused like a student who cannot comprehend the message; keep your paragraphs short and to the point.

Also, be mindful that your audience might include people whose native language isn't English, so write for them as well.

Use certain jargon properly

If your content is geared toward a specific audience, ensure that you have used terms properly. If you are unsure, ask questions as well as ask someone to examine what you have written. Do not post anything that experts in the field can read and know that you are inexperienced about the topic. For example, if you have a business geared toward teenagers but you write the content with slang that has been out of rotation since the 1970s, teenagers reading the information will be clueless about what you are saying.

Nonetheless, just because it is jargon and you are catering to your audience, doesn't mean that you should use a lot of it. If a newbie clicks on your site and sees certain expressions, they should still be able to follow and understand what you have written.

Spell out acronyms

If you have spelled it out in a paragraph before, there is nothing wrong with using acronyms thereafter. In addition, some acronyms are easy to follow based on the context. For example, on your blog you might say:

I had an addiction with alcohol. I finally went to an AA meeting and there I met the CEO of my daughter's company.

Readers will be able to follow what AA and CEO mean should you opt not to spell out the terms. However, you may induce a headache if it reads like this:

The other day I went to Starbucks and met my computer programmer who is from UGT. I was sharing with him my VBN challenges and he advised that I used the PBC, and the HJI more than the KOT for my business to WDC.

Do not be alarmed. I am just using the letters to illustrate that you should not write as if you are talking in code. You are writing for human beings. If the letters have a meaning, spell out what they mean so you do not leave your audience confused and bewildered.

Use numbers in your headlines

Research reveals that when you use numbers in your headlines, more people will click through to see the content. You do not have to include it only in the body of your content.

Moreover, odd numbers have more impact than even numbers.

7 superfoods to boost your energy.

101 ways to lose weight.

Appropriately use threats or persuade readers to support a cause

In real life, you know the power of emotions and the fear of one's health and safety being threatened.

For example, the kitchen needs cleaning. The car needs cleaning, too. The children spilled something sticky on floor. They tried cleaning it up but made a bigger mess instead. It's Saturday, your day off and you really can't be bothered. You curl deeper under the covers. You are happy, your children are safe, and life is good. You hear them laughing in the next room, and you laugh too. Then you receive a text message from a friend saying that the food you bought last week has been recalled because of contamination. You fly out of the bedroom and in one hour you have rushed your children to the doctor for a checkup just to be on the safe side, super cleaned the entire house, thrown out the recalled food, and cleaned the car.

Do not underestimate the power of threats and emotions. However, do not use them ignorantly. You are not one of those tabloids. Use this tactic in good taste. Once you have used this strategy appropriately, you will have more clicks than you ever imagined and you'll have readers doing what you would like them to do.

Look at this example.

Concerned about your health? Implement these 5 home remedies to quickly rid your home of mosquitoes.

In these times, who doesn't want to eliminate mosquitoes from their home?

Other provocative words are beware, danger, jeopardy, and risk.

The example Concerned about your health? Implement these 5 home remedies to quickly rid your home of mosquitoes, also exemplifies the use of questions, numbers and power words in the headlines.

I emphasize again the importance of using this tactic properly. Your goal is to increase your credibility and make your audience feel that you are genuinely concerned about them. Having your audience living in fear and playing with their emotions is not a good behavior for a content marketer who wants to be trusted. If you keep doing this, after a while your readers will see right through your charade. Make sure that you have worded your material so that you offer solutions and highlight what they can do to make things better.

Do not have a vague call to action

A call to action (CTA) is an instruction to your audience asking that they perform a specific action.

Be concise and write with clarity when giving a directive to your audience. You do not want 500 of your readers to email you and all are asking the same question. What exactly am I to do? In fact, you may be lucky if they even take the time to email you with their queries. The odds are that they will just click on someone else's website whose call to action is clearer.

Using the example of the herbal teas in India that we mentioned before, after reading about the journey and how you lost 250 pounds, what do you want the audience to do next? Nothing?

Or do you want them to sign up to receive free samples of the herbal tea? Or do you want them to pay to receive a month's worth of tea? Or do you want them to only share their stories of what dietary methods worked for them?

Be very clear so that your readers understand what they should do after reading your content. You can also put the CTA inside a button or banner so it can be very prominent for your audience to notice it.

Have you ever signed up for something and there is a message that it will take 3 steps, then on step 1 there is a button that says Next and an arrow next to it? Everything is properly laid out. Have the same organization where everything can be followed on your site.

Give free trials

I am not in any way asking you to put your business in jeopardy by reducing profits. If a new bakery opened up and you are looking for someone to cater, you may think about using the services as the pastries are lovely. However, you may hesitate because though they make one particular item well, you are not sure about the other items. You want to sample and observe what others are saying before you make that commitment.

It is the same thing with your business. Your readers have their lives and budgets. Although your offerings are wonderful, they want to be sure that they are doing the right thing and will get value for their money. To help them along, offer them a sample or a free trial, or give free demonstrations.

You do not necessarily have to give a 30-day or 60-day trial period like other big companies do. You know your objectives and what is best for you, so only you can set the time period. You do not have to include the words Buy!

Buy! Buy! Placing them three times on every page on your website to encourage people to purchase what you have to offer isn't necessary. A trial period can work wonders for you.

You are telling your viewers that your brand is so good, you don't mind them testing it to see just how great it is.

Repurpose your material

Was one of your blog posts so good that 7 months later, the comments still keep coming in? The thread is very long and you have received great commendations. Why not reword that post? Or use the information in another format? You can use videos and audio to highlight the same thing.

Not every post has to tell a story

Storytelling is one way to convey your work, but it is not the only way. Do not get caught in thinking that every blog post has to tell a story. If that is what you prefer, there is nothing wrong with using what works for you. However, if you are not a natural storyteller, do not be bogged down with something that you do not prefer.

Be controversial

If you are not comfortable with controversy, by all means invite a guest blogger or hire someone to write your content. When you take a controversial stance, it causes a reaction. Do so tastefully, as you do not want to alienate potential customers by saying something so outrageous that even your friends wonder if they really know you. Remember your aim is to be credible, not irrational, so choose your topics wisely and strike an appropriate balance.

Include keywords

Web pages and the information on them are ranked on search engines. This is called Search Engine Optimization (SEO) and it is a way to acquire more traffic. People around the world research certain topics. If one of your key words is a word they are looking for, your website will be listed according to how it is ranked. Include more key words in your headlines and content.

Imagine that you went to Brazil five years ago and you created a blog post during the Olympics. You created a blog post with the heading My Trip Abroad. What is so special about your trip abroad that will make strangers want to read about it? Many people were keying in Rio in the search engines, wanting to know more about the people and the culture. If you're heading was Rio: The most splendid time of my life, that would guarantee to have more people clicking on the link when it pops up in the search engines. It would have many more hits than My Trip Abroad. Therefore, be mindful of the impact that keywords have.

Follow the best bloggers

You can get inspiration from looking at other blogs. However, be mindful of the blogs you follow. Just because a company is huge and may be one of your favorite companies, does not necessarily mean that they are successful with content marketing. This is so because some corporate blogs find it difficult to harmonize their voice with their brand. Some companies are accustomed to the traditional ways of marketing and content marketing is a new process to them.

On the other hand, superstars and other celebrities who blog have mastered the art because their brand is a reflection of who they are. They do not struggle to find their voice. They are as personable as when you see them in concerts, on the television, or wherever they make appearances. Although you may follow corporate blogs, make sure that they are successful in content marketing and their voice complements their brand. Do not follow the wrong bloggers and make the same mistakes that they are making.

Answer complicated questions

Do you remember those random quizzes in school? When it's your turn, you hope that the teacher will ask you a question that you know the answer to. You can see the look of despair on your classmates' faces. Everyone looks doomed. It's your turn, and you brace yourself and the teacher asks you the most complicated question of all. The class waits with bated breath, as they are sure you are about to faint from the enormity of the question. Even the teacher smirks.

Triumphantly and confidently you tell her the answer to the size of the moon. The teacher looks like she is about to faint. You even tell her about the galaxies and all the information you know from that Discovery Channel documentary you watched. Your classmates look at you in awe. They didn't know you were so intelligent. You thank your lucky stars.

Who doesn't want to know the answer to complicated questions? People do not have the time to research in this busy world. They may have it in their minds that one day they will find the answer to the burning questions they have, but something always stops them.

You can help your audience by answering complex questions. You may wonder, like what? What field are you in? What is your business about? What are your objectives? Are you into investments? Real estate? Have you been in the business for a while, or are you new to it? What are some of the frequently asked questions in your particular industry? What are some of the things that customers are concerned about? Answer them. Make things easier for your customers.

Chapter 3

Social Media

You can use Facebook, Twitter, LinkedIn, and YouTube which are the main ones and thesocial media platforms, as well as other forms of social media at your disposal. Social media is used to distribute your material to an audience.

Select the right movers and shakers

When launching a service or product on social media, you can research and find the right influencer who has said something on the same topic or related topics. In this way, your audience can identify more with the information you have posted.

For example, if your product helps to get rid of wrinkles and a celebrity or influential journalist has reported on the same topic, mention it along with the information you have posted.

Spot opportunities from other people's mistakes

You should pay attention to what your competitors are saying and doing, to capitalize on certain opportunities. For example, if your competitor sells female products geared toward women and the chairman of the company saidmade some harsh statements about womenmisogynistic comments, you do not have to wait on the angry comments from women to know what will happen next. Position your brand and enhance your content, letting readers know that you value women. When the competitor's audience seek for alternatives, it will be easy for them to find yours.

You cannot spot real -time opportunities by only waiting for the news to be reported in your newspaper or on the television. Social media is where you can get current information. Therefore, use it to your advantage.

It does not even have to be a competitor,; it can be something that is in the news. For example, let's assume that a recall was made to a particular anti-aging skin cream. You can provide an article about why products get recalled or alternatives to anti-aging cream. Know what is trending and write valuable material that your audience will appreciate.

Be careful with the images you use

Social media is very dynamic. The attention span of your audience is not like the generation before. The average attention span online is just a few seconds. Make sure that the images you use and headlines you use are attention - grabbing.

Let's assume that something happened in the news and you wish to write about it. Be selective with the images you post. Let's assume that you decided to "swipe" a picture from the competitor. After all, the post had 11 images and you have none. Who will find out? Everything seems fine, people are clicking on your link until someone asks, "Is this the same story or a different story because X newsfeed has that same story and picture."?" Your audience then goes to X postsX's post, and you are exposed. You try to explain that it is your story. You wrote it from scratch. However, you may have some skeptics because there is the proof of you swiping the same picture. They may wonder if in fact you swiped the article from some other source or whether it is originally your story. Be very careful about where you source you pictures.

Links

Do your links lead your audience to the correct landing page? Perhaps you made some changes to your website and forgot to use the right link. You post something on social media with the old link. Sign Upup by clicking the link. Your audience clicks the link not just once, but several times. Either the link is incorrect or if it works, they are directed to your photo gallery page on your website instead of the correct page. Test your links before posting them.

Use the right tone

Do not write as if it is you versus them. Your tone should not sound standoffish or condescending. Make sure you use the correct pronouns so that it sounds more personable. Write as if you are having a conversation, soand avoid the formality.

For example, on your blog you may sound so down to earth and on other platforms you sound like an austere school teacher. This may happen when you have different people creating your content and managing your various platforms. Ensure that you have the right team and the right people are assigned to various tasks. Your audience should be made to feel like you are speaking with one voice, so ensure that your content, wherever it is distributed, correlates.

Chapter 4

Expand Your Horizons

Bon Appétit

Bon Appétit is an entertainment magazine that was launched in 1955. Its sister publication was Gourmet magazine, which was first published in 1941. The last issue was in 2009. The Gourmet brand is still used for certain topics, although the magazine no longer exists.

Bon Appétit started a podcast campaign in November 2014 entitled the "Bon Appétit Foodcast." The length of the podcast is 30 minutes. Some of the top guests that were featured include Mark Bittman, Ina Garten, and Gordon Ramsay.

Mark Bittman is a food journalist who has written more than 10 books. He is regularly featured on NBC's The Today Show and other popular television programs. Ina Garten, an American, has a program on the Food Network, several cookbooks, and specializes in French cuisine.

Gordon Ramsay, OBE, was born in Scotland and raised in England. He has several restaurants and they have all been highly commended. Ramsay is known for his fiery outbursts, tough criticisms, and wisecracks on popular food programs. Forbes named him as the 21st highest money-making celebrity in the world. Some of the programs in which he is featured include Hell's Kitchen, Hotel Hell, Ramsay's Kitchen Nightmares, and MasterChef.

Members of staff have also been featured on the podcast. This is a list of some episodes that were featured in 2014 and 2015:

The Ultimate Guide to Thanksgiving
It's All About the Holidays
Let's get Healthy(ish)
Get Your Super Bowl Party On
On Valentine's Day... and Mexican Food
Comfort Food and the State of the Drinking World
The Waffle House, Vegetable Restaurants, and Baking Tips
Make a Better Salad, Food Binge in Las Vegas
Never Mess Up Eggs Again, Editor-In-Chief Smackdown
Food Superstars Ina Garten & Gordon Ramsey

Some of the 2016 episodes are:

It's Not Valentine's Day Without Molten Chocolate Cake

We're Going Retro

City of Jonathan Gold

Action Bronson

Podcasting was not available years before. However, today it is a popular way of distributing information and it is a widely accepted medium for sharing audio files. A great way to improve your credibility is to have experts and other great guests talk about what they are passionate about.

Do not limit yourself or think that it is impossible to get an expert. Every friend has a friend. When you network effectively, you will be surprised at the people who you can feature on your podcast.

Jack Daniel Whiskey

Jack Daniel was founded by Jasper Newton "Jack" Daniel in Lynchburg, Tennessee in 1875.

Jack was born in the late 1840s. His father remarried and later died in the Civil War and Jack ran away as he didn't get along with his stepmother. He was given a place to stay by a distiller and lay preacher called Dan Call. He learned the trade from Dan and an enslaved African who was the master distiller.

Jack inherited money from his dad's estate and established his business. Jack obtained a gold medal from the St. Louis World's Fair for his whiskey in 1904. A law was passed and it was unlawful to distil Jack Daniel in that state. Operations began in other states.

Today, there are many Jack Daniel competitions, such as Jack Daniel's MasterGriller Competition and Jack Daniel's Smokin' Grills BBQ Competition. These competitions are based on how whiskey can be used in cooking. Jack Daniel's blog connects with their audience by providing information on food that can be consumed while enjoying a bottle Jack Daniel's.

Also, on the Jack Daniel's Facebook page they allow their audience to create their own labels. You can create several labels per month.

You can host competitions and let your brand be more visible. Additionally, you can provide trivia on your blog about various popular brands. If your blog is about liquor, for example, rather than have generic information, include entertaining trivia that your audience may not be aware of. Using our Jack Daniel example, trivia that can be included on a blog dedicated to liquor can include:

The county where Jack Daniel whiskey is produced is a dry county. A dry county means that selling alcoholic drinks is forbidden.

Though Jack Daniel is over 140 years old, there have been fewer than 10 Master Distillers. These are the people who maintain that quality of the product using the techniques that were first implemented in the late 1800s.

This is an example, but you can include trivia that will make you sound like an expert in your particular industry.

Hipmunk

Hipmunk is an online travel company based in San Francisco, California. It was established in 2010.

It provides search results to an online audience and ranks flights by price, schedule, and challenges. The latter is based on the length of the flight and the stops that one has to endure if one opts to take that flight.

In addition, information about Amtrak train routes and places to spend the night are given. Hipmunk receives a commission from flight companies, hotels, and other related sites that the company promotes.

In 2011, the company developed an iPhone app. That same year they exceeded one million search queries on a monthly basis. They were named by Time magazine as one of the 50 Best Websites of 2011.

Hipmunk provides extra content for travelers, such as information about tipping in various countries, things to do in a particular place, and information about taxis and places to eat.

What Hipmunk has done is provide the answers to questions in a comprehensive format. Readers do not have to find the answers elsewhere. The information is valuable and essential for travelers. When Hipmunk first launched, their objective was to be the leader in the industry even though there were others in the field. They pulled out all the stops to attract their competitors' audience as well as new customers. In 2015, they launched innovative Facebook campaigns. In addition, the company was able to raise $6 million in venture funding in April 2016.

You can be new in your field and still dominate. It is not about when you started but how effective your strategy is. You have to ensure that you evaluate your objectives and goals and find the best ways to attain them.

American Express

As of 2016, American Express has been operating for 166 years having first been established in 1850. It is also referred to as Amex and is known for its charge cards, credit cards, and traveler's checks business. In 2011, Fortune magazine included it in the top 20 Most Admired Companies in the World.

Ogilvy & Mather, the marketing and communication giant, produced the popular ad campaign in 1975. The popular slogan is, "Don't Leave Home Without It." In 2004, another brand campaign was launched and the slogan is, "My life. My card." Over the years, the ad has featured celebrities such as Venus Williams, Robert De Niro, Ellen DeGeneres, and Martin Scorsese.

American Express has been one of the companies who has used cause marketing. What is cause marketing? Also referred to as cause-related marketing, it is one type of marketing where a for profit entity and a non-profit entity cooperate for a charitable or social cause.

In Chapter 2, we discussed this topic: Appropriately use threats or persuade readers to support a cause.

I used the example of the parent who was told that the food she bought had been recalled and how that made her rush out of bed to sort out her children's health and organize her home. In the other example, we also used the threat of mosquitoes to persuade readers to try the 5 home remedies to get rid of mosquitoes.

In this chapter, we will examine how American Express used a cause to promote their brand. As far back as 1983, the company informed the public that for every purchase that was transacted with an American Express card, the company would contribute one penny to the repairs of the Statue of Liberty. Just under $2 million dollars was raised. There was a 28% increase in the card's usage during that campaign.

This is one way you can increase your credibility. Be genuine in your cause. If you engage in underhanded dealings, it will ruin your business and your reputation. Referring to one of our examples, if you ask your audience to buy packets of your tea, you can let them know a percentage of the profits will be used toward a cause.

You have to be transparent. Do not take the money and buy another ticket to India and have your audience wondering what happened to the cause. It is your reputation on the line, so be prudent.

Global Business Travel Association is a travel management organization. Its original name was National Business Travel Association before the name change in 2011. It was established in 1968.

In 2015, American Express teamed up with Global Business Travel Association and produced a report on business travelers and their level of satisfaction. There were blog posts, event presentations, and other related content about technology and expense management.

This is another way to increase your credibility. Partner with a company or someone who is a giant in the industry. Do research and produce reports that an audience will appreciate.

Chapter 5

The Value of Listening to Your Audience

One way to increase your credibility is doing everything that you can to eradicate any negativity surrounding your content.

If someone shares his or her opinion about your content in a respectful manner, that is great because it keeps the conversation interesting and engaging. Furthermore, there will be criticisms and harsh comments from internet trolls who can be very disrespectful, but you have all the strategies on how to deflect them as we have previously examined this topic. However, when someone shares his or her awful experience while interacting with you or your staff or while using your product or service, it can be detrimental to your business if it is not addressed immediately.

The avenue for eliminating and minimizing negative feedback and reviews is through customer service. You may wonder, how is customer service relevant in content marketing?

Let us complete an exercise. Reflect on the worst customer experience that you had. If you have a difficult time brainstorming, allow me to help you. Was a sales clerk very impolite? Did you have to wait for 35 minutes at a restaurant before someone took your order? After waiting for 40 minutes for your food, was it different from what you had ordered? Did the waitress scream at you? When you called customer service for help about installing a product, did the representative yell at you and hang up before you could finish explaining?

After your horrible experience, what did you do? Did you smile and ignore it? Or did you tell your friends and family about it? Did you discourage people from conducting any transaction with that particular business where you had your awful experience? Did you write about it in social media? If you did, realize that it is the same thing that will happen when members of your audience are disrespected and disregarded. Some of your customers may not even complain; they will just refuse to conduct business with you ever again. Can you really afford to lose customers after diligently marketing your content?

The Value of Listening to Your Audience

Customer Service is an integral part of successful content marketing. It is not only about minimizing bad reviews and complaints; it's also about providing clarification for your customers. Customer Service sometimes gets relegated to the back burner while you attempt to sift through the plethora of content to market your company the best way you know how. However, Customer Service plays a pivotal role in your company's growth and how you interact with your audience.

Customer Service is taking care of your customers by providing professional and helpful assistance so that their needs are met. Remember that content marketing is about providing value to your customers. It is better to provide good service from the beginning rather than trying to correct mistakes after an incident occurs. Your credibility can be undermined by disgruntled customers with the click of a button in a few seconds. Today, customers are sharing their grievances in public forums and social media platforms.

Below are some important tips on how to improve your great standing with customers. The attributes of customer service include delivering assistance that is:

Timely

Being prompt with the delivery of a service is very important. Long delays and cancellations can be very frustrating to your customers. This may cause them to take their business elsewhere.

Attentive

You have to listen to your customers. If you are looking at them, if you are in person, or if you have the phone to your ear, do not focus your thoughts on what you will eat for dinner. Then when the customer asks a question you repeat, "Can you repeat what you just said?" Be mindful and focus.

Polite

Use politeness when serving customers. "Good afternoon," "Hello," and "Thank you," can always brighten someone's day. Even if you do get a response in return, it is part of serving others. You have to remain professional at all times.

Communication Skills

You may be a great blogger. Your stories may have enabled you to receive attention from all over the world. You are a great storyteller. However, in customer service you need communication skills. Your storytelling expertise will not help 100% with interacting with customers. It may assist you, but it won't solve the problem.

For example, let us assume that you sell pet products. A customer comes into your business place and informs you that she ordered a brown collar online but your business sent her a red one instead and she doesn't like the color red. She shows you a receipt of what she ordered online and a picture of her cat wearing a brown collar. She explains that it is a picture of the old collar and she wanted one exactly like that.

Rather than addressing her issue with the wrong delivery, you talk about your own cat, Tabby, discussing all these adorable stories about how you adopted her. How does this help resolve the issue in a timely manner?

Furthermore, if you have staff members, make sure you let them know if they are unsure about something, to first ask a question rather than miscommunicating to customers.

Let's assume that another customer called and said she surfed online and saw a red collar that she would like for her dog. She sees that it says "temporarily out of stock." She calls and inquires when the stock will be replenished. Rather than finding out the correct information, your staff member says, "Tomorrow." The red collars are not scheduled to arrive until next month.

Be careful with communication. It will be unfortunate to spend so much time creating your content and marketing it and at the point where the customer is ready to purchase or has purchased, the service is so poor that the customers goes somewhere else to conduct business or asks for a refund.

Knowledge of Service or Product

Your employees must be aware and have a deep understanding of what you provide. Can you imagine that you have created wonderful content, there are thousands of likes on Facebook, people are retweeting you on Twitter, you have thousands of views on YouTube, other bloggers are raving about your content, and when customers call or send an email your staff says something like, "Huh?" or "I don't know. I'm not really sure." Or even more detrimental, "Can you call back…like… next week?"

Personable

If you know a customer's name, use it. Even if you don't know their name, you can ask for a name. Rather than saying, "Miss, we do not have this product," it is so much more pleasant to say, "Mary Jane, unfortunately we do not have this product. However, we have an alternative. Let me show you." You should be warm and engaging, not cold and blunt.

Use the Right Language

You should convey positive messages to your customers. Your tone and that of your employees must be cordial and positive. Phrases like "Yep I think so," "I don't know," and

"Whatever" is the language of people who are not serious about improving the business.

Patient

Yes, I'll admit, it is not easy working with irate customers. However, it is important to maintain your patience with them. By getting upset, you only tend to exacerbate the customer's emotions. Calm down and try your best to be helpful.

Body Language

If a customer comes to your business or if there is a video chat feature, use the right body language. Rolling of the eyes, hands on hips like you are ready to fight, and other similar stances can make your customers feel like they are wasting their time.

Professional

Always remember that it is a business you have, and treat your customers professionally. Give them the best service so that they will return and also tell their friends and family about what you have to offer.

Have a Calming Demeanor

You can be patient, but your face actually looks menacing. The customer is unsure if they should bother voicing their concerns or if they should just walk out of the store. Relax your face and try your best to create a calming atmosphere. It may even involve asking a customer to have seat, rather than standing. You can offer them water or whatever is necessary to calm customers down if they are upset.

Ability to Handle the Unexpected

You and your staff must be able to handle any surprises that may come your way, especially when it is something you didn't even imagine would happen to you. You should be able to think on your feet or prepare the words you or your staff should say when a situation arises.

Let us assume that you sell a product called Smooth and Lovely. A customer visits your store and complains that the Lovely cream made her break out with a rash. She shows you and you are stunned. Will you scream for other customers to hear, "Oh no! That means everyone who buys the cream will have a rash!!! That looks awful!!!! I've never seen this type of reaction to the skin cream we sell!" By this time, other customers are drawing closer to see and hear properly. Will you give the customer a full refund, the fee to see the doctor, and shut the entire store down for the day?

The first step should be to get to the root of the situation by having a private conversation, and do not panic.

What if after listening attentively, you realize that the customer made a mistake. Your product is called Smooth and Lovely. She bought a product called Fair and Lovely. It was when she showed you the cream and the invoice that you realized that this was not your product but something else that she bought online.

Can you imagine how you would have lost customers if you had panicked and didn't handle the situation properly? What if you had shut down the entire store for the day and lost hundreds of dollars because you didn't listen and ask the appropriate questions? Have systems in place where your staff is trained to handle certain scenarios, and if they are unsure, let them know who to refer the issue to.

Let us examine some examples of wonderful customer satisfaction.

Good Examples

Morton's The Steakhouse

Morton's The Steakhouse was established in 1978 in Chicago, Illinois. Currently there are approximately 70 chain restaurants. In 2011, Landry acquired ownership of The Steakhouse. The company's head offices were relocated to Houston, Texas.

Some of the marketing campaigns that they are known for are "Lunch with a Legend" where customers dine with athletes. They also have "Celebrity Server" where celebrities perform waiter duties at events that are hosted to raise funds for charities and foundations.

A customer by the name of Peter was awaiting his flight in Florida. As a joke, he asked if the restaurant could deliver a porterhouse steak to the airport so he could have it as soon as he arrived. He expressed that he would land 2 hours later. To Peter's surprise, when he arrived at his destination in Newark, a server from Morton's The Steakhouse was there to deliver his steak, bread, potatoes, and shrimp.

How much do you think that Peter had to pay for that type of delivery? Nothing. It was absolutely free. Imagine that the order was sent all the way to the airport and in return there was no price. Peter was shocked, but the promotion that the restaurant received when Peter posted it on social media was more than worth the trip.

When you surprise customers in a nice way, you can surely make warm memories. Of course, you cannot give your profit away if you are not a huge company like the restaurant. However, you can find simple and creative ways to surprise your customers.

Waterstones

Waterstones is a bookstore in London, United Kingdom that was established in 1982. There are approximately 275 stores with just under 4000 employees. Surveys have been done by the public who ranked various businesses according to the level of customer satisfaction they have received, and on those occasions, the bookstore raked within the top ten.

A shopper was locked inside a bookstore by accident. He tweeted asking to be let out. He had over 16,000 retweets and more than 12,000 likes. Someone was actively checking the Twitter feed and was able to resolve the problem by opening the store.

The company responded by tweeting that the man was free and thanked the customers for the concern. Monitoring your customers' comments does not end when employees leave the office. What if the Waterstones' employee who was assigned to check the comments had decided not to monitor what was happening? Always be attuned to what is happening, even after usual business hours.

Nike

Nike has customer support every day of the week and in seven foreign languages.

A customer asked for help in allocating his order number. After much exchange, the customer realized that he had the information all along. Nike responded respectfully and told the customer he was free to contact the company again if he had any other problems. It was the customer's fault, yet the representative was very kind. It is very important to be courteous.

Gaylord Opryland Resort

Gaylord Opryland Resort is located in Nashville, Tennessee. Previously, it was called Opryland Hotel Nashville and had the name change in 2001.

A guest by the name of Christina was staying at the resort. She fell in love with the radio clock that was placed in her room. There was a sound feature on the clock that made her rest better than she had for a long time. She inquired about where she could purchase one just like it. However, the clock was an exclusive product of the resort and there was no store where she could purchase it.

When she returned to her room, there was gift. Inside was a handwritten note and a clock. Christina became a loyal customer and the hotel received a lot of coverage for the staff's kind gesture.

Delta Hotel

Another guest by the name of Mike was a guest of Delta Hotel. He enjoyed the amenities in his room, but the view wasn't pleasant at all. He did not include the hotel in his post. He was just venting and posted on social media that he didn't like the view. In one hour, the hotel was able to respond. This means that someone was monitoring the comments on social media.

One hour later, the manager, offered him a better room on his next trip and a dish filled with treats along with a handwritten note. The hotel representative apologized that he was unable to place Mike on another floor but it was due to the level of occupancy as the hotel was full. Mike followed up and wrote about his great experience.

Trader Joe's

Trader Joe's has more than 450 stores and is known for its organic and fresh foods. It was established in 1958 and was called Pronto Market. In 1967 it changed the name to Trader Joe's.

During the Christmas holidays, a daughter of an 89-year-old man called several places hoping to find one that could deliver food to her father as he was snowed in. She was concerned that he wouldn't have enough food during the dreadful weather. She called several places, but had no luck. She finally called Trader Joe's and was informed that they do not deliver. Nonetheless, because of the critical situation, they arranged for the deliveries to be made. They also recommended items that he would enjoy as he needed to consume foods with low sodium levels. The delivery was free of charge and the father received the delivery in half an hour.

Starbucks

Starbucks was established in 1971 in Washington. Today, there are just under 25,000 worldwide locations. Starbucks has received over 200,000 ideas.

A great way to improve your business is by listening to what customers have to impart.

Bad Examples

Scenario 1

A customer has a problem and calls customer service, hoping to be enlightened as to what to do. The representative gets defensive and says, "There is nothing wrong with our product!" The customer goes on to mention that it is not doing what the instructions say should be happening. The representative then tells the customer things like, "It's your fault. Your probably can't follow instructions." When the customer asks to speak to someone else, the representative hangs up.

Scenario 2

Another response to a customer: "Our policy clearly states that there is no refund and no, I'm not letting you speak to the supervisor!"

The Value of Listening to Your Audience

Scenario 3

A customer asks a question about a food item. He wants to know where he can find them in a supermarket. The employee then responds, "Do you think you should be eating those? You need to lose a lot of weight and they will make you fatter."

Scenario 4

A man passed away and his daughter called a credit card agency to terminate his account. She informed the representative the reason she was canceling the account was because her father was dead. The representative told the daughter that before he could do anything further, he would need to speak to her father.

Make sure that your customer representative listens to everything that is said. The customer was so angry that the supervisor had to be called to resolve the situation.

Scenario 5

A customer calls with a problem and is placed on hold for almost an hour. After waiting, for the situation is very urgent, he is told, "Looks like we can't help you after all!"

Scenario 6

A customer gets to the cash register with money in hand to pay the price she saw on the rack next to the item. When she gets to the cashier, another price rings up. The customer asks about the discrepancy and the cashier tells her, "It's what's in the system." The customer asks to speak to someone else and the cashier ignores her and says, "Are you ready to pay?" to the customer behind of her. In the cashier's world, the customer has become invisible and no longer exists.

Scenario 7

A customer calls to speak to someone who can help him and he is greeted with a foreign accent. He hangs up and thinks that he called the wrong company. He checks the number and dials it. A representative who cannot speak English properly, speaks fluently in her native language. In his frustration, he hangs up.

If you are going to have customer support, make sure that there is someone suitable who can understand and respond appropriately to queries.

The Correlation Between Customer Service and Content Marketing

There are several reasons why it is important to have a proper nexus between content marketing and customer service. Below are the main reasons.

Improves Your Support System on Social Media

The person who manages your social media should have appropriate customer service skills. It is more than posting your content in the newsfeed and checking to see how many likes you have obtained and how many times it was shared. Technology has changed the way that customers reach businesses and companies. One comment can go viral. Therefore, someone should be checking the page and also know how to respond appropriately.

You can also have staff from other departments be involved in examining the social page. Content marketing on social media does not have to be caged into one department. Customer service is everyone's job. If someone from another department sees something, the matter should be brought to the attention of the relevant managers. Your staff should not be of the mindset that the matter should only be addressed during working hours. For example, if a customer makes a complaint on the page and your staff sees it five minutes after working hours, he or she should not let it wait until next morning at 9 a.m. One of the key requirements of customer service is timely response.

Obtain Ideas

If you are experiencing problems with finding content, you can get ideas by interacting more with your customers. Those in customer service will be the ones resolving problems, answering queries, and guiding customers along.

You can engage your customer service staff to get ideas for your next topic.

Additionally, you can provide information by finding out what customers want the answers to and compiling them in a Frequently Asked Questions content. While you are busy sourcing information for your content, do not overlook your customer service representatives.

Helps to Meet the Expectations of Your Customers

Your customers will have their expectations and by improving your customer service relations, you will ensure that many of their concerns are settled. When your marketing representatives and your customer service representatives are suitably working together, a marketer can adapt or amend certain campaigns and correct any errors and inconsistencies.

Let's revisit the example above with the skin cream Smooth & Lovely. Once the customer representative reports the incident to management or the marketing team, the content can be modified where it educates the public about the different ingredients that are used to make your product as opposed to those in other products. Moreover, you may let the public know what to do if they have sensitive skin.

Makes a Stronger Team

Usually the first stop when a customer has a concern is the customer support, so you should also ensure that your customer representative knows about the campaign you are running and/or the contest that is on social media platforms.

Let us assume that a customer calls and inquires about a campaign from your customer representative. The customer asks, "Will you have a contest every month?" and your rep answers, "Huh? What contest?" The customer may respond, "The one on Facebook." Then your rep answers, "Are you sure? I don't know anything about that. Perhaps you're mistaken."

That conversation will totally topple your credibility.

Improves Your Customer Happiness

The purpose of your content is to provide value to your customers. By ensuring that your customer service team and marketing team communicate more and are better informed about what is happening, it ensures that your customer will have a happier experience. It is a matter of turning anger and discontentment to smiles and a better customer experience. For those customers who are already satisfied, surprise them. They will be so appreciative of what you have done, that they will have no choice but to share the experience.

Understanding Personas

A persona profile is an outline of your ideal buyer. It is a profile that you sketch. You can get a deeper knowledge of your persona by interacting more with your customers and listening to their complaints, concerns, reviews, and general feedback.

Campaigns to help with personas

If you have been in business for some time, perhaps you have been producing campaign after campaign, yet you're not seeing the results that you would like. You have lost sleep to produce more content, installed a fancy design on your website, designed more landing pages, and shared a lot on various social media platforms. When you look at campaigns produced by other companies, they are doing well. Yet you are unsure as to what to do to see better results.

You have to know the market you are in. For example, if you are selling whole grain crackers, you cannot compare your campaigns with another business who is selling potato chips and chocolate cakes. You can't compare campaigns to those of a business selling hair products. Every market is different, and so should your strategy be. You must have a clear picture as to who makes up your audience.

The Value of Listening to Your Audience

Look at your data. You can have a survey. Create a form and ask certain questions. You can add other information if you wish, but these basic queries will help you to obtain the information you require.

The form can include:
- First name and last name
- Email address
- Job role
- Previous positions held
- Whether the customer has a degree
- Favorite website or blog that is used to obtain information about their pertinent industry
- Events attended in the past 2 years

You will need to ascertain who is reaching out to you. Who are you serving with your content? You will know what your strengths are and capitalize on them.

For example, perhaps in your business of selling whole grain crackers, your persona was that most of the members of your audience were people trying to lose weight when in actuality your audience is made up of people with a specific health condition who were purchasing your item.

Once you know who you are targeting, then you can properly adjust your content. Look at your data and determine which topics received the most hits. For example, perhaps your content was about aerobics and losing weight, but it generated low traffic. You can repurpose the information and also explore topics about people with specific health conditions. You may even decide to offer other food items. You can then begin to strategize more effectively.

Chapter 6

Personal Advancement

Be honest with yourself

You can only advance in business more rapidly according to how properly you establish credibility with your customers, investors, and other colleagues. You can do everything that was outlined in the previous chapters, but if you do not take the time to develop your interpersonal skills, change old mindsets, and have a practical outlook, your growth and reputation will move at a slower pace.

Be genuine about what you do. That is why it is very important to know what your objectives are and use them as a guideline. You should be in the industry that you are really passionate about. In that way, when you feel stuck, you will know that it is only for a time or a phase. When you are passionate about something, there is always some form of inspiration to get you up and moving again. For example, if your blog caters to diet and exercise only because you feel that it is the trend and that is where you can make your money, but in your heart, you find it dull and boring, then your content and your attitude will reflect how you feel. Perhaps you can mask it for a while. However, eventually your feelings will be revealed.

What if you have videos on your blog of you engaging in exercise? Perhaps when you started, you thought the profits would be rolling in, so you were energized while doing your aerobics. You encouraged you audience to join you three times a week as both of you commit to living healthier lives. Six months later, when the money is not rolling in, you reduce your videos to once per week. Yet instead of you smiling and feeling energized as you do your workouts, you grunt and sigh and look as if you are being tortured. Frankly, you dislike exercise and your mind is on the junk food you have in the kitchen. Don't you think your audience will know that you are not enthused by what you do? So how can you expect them to buy your product or service?

Remember that you are not just reaching out to an audience in other parts of the world; there are people in your community who know you and interact with you. You may be credible online, but in your neck of the woods how do people view you? It is very important to listen to your inner thoughts and do the things that you are really interested in doing. What if you prefer to have a blog dedicated to cooking? Why not do so, rather than having a blog about exercise? You can look for healthier ingredients in your recipes. Look at all your options.

Be honest with others

When you tell lies, you have to remember everything you said and when you said it. Telling lies also causes people to distrust you.

Let us assume that you tell a customer that a new replacement will be in the mail when you know for a fact you have no intention of sending anything. When the customer calls back later in the week and you take the call, you change your voice and say that perhaps it was a member of your staff who told her that, but your company will not be able to send a replacement. What if one of your staff members overhears the conversation? How would you feel? Be conscious of what you say and do.

Know the value of your service/product

When you are aware of the true value of what you have, you can communicate to one person passionately or speak to 1,000 with the same amount of fervor. Sometimes people do not know the value of something unless you tell them and show them.

You cannot expect people to know what you are thinking; you have to communicate with them. Even if they have their doubts, you have to influence and persuade them. Do not dupe anyone. If you are selling a product and you know that after 3 months the product will stop working but you don't care because by then the warranty will have expired, do you think it is as easy as moving right along? That could have happened years ago. You could have rolled into a state selling worthless goods with a horse and carriage and moved on to the next state, but not now. Things have changed, and so should your mindset.

Be confident

If you are just starting your business, do not feel discouraged. Every big business started somewhere. You have to maintain your level of confidence no matter how it looks or what people may say. That is why you must know the value of what you have to offer and be honest with yourself, as these factors can chip away your confidence.

Once you are certain that you are doing what you really want to do, and you know what your objectives are and you have a great strategy in place, keep positive and confident. The more confident you are, the more people will be persuaded to support what you do.

Listen and respond appropriately

If you are a sole proprietor, this is very important. Businesses who have staff and employees can delegate. When it is you alone, you have to listen and respond properly.

There will be the naysayers, the internet trolls are lurking and waiting to attack, but you have to train yourself how to respond. You are only human and you will take it personally. However, you have to know how to respond to the negative things that are said. "Thank you," or "I will look into the matter immediately," can go a longer way than cursing everyone out on your blog.

Be sensitive

You must exhibit empathy for your staff or team members and customers. Fully understand their desires and appreciate their background and their contributions.

Have a shared vision

If you work as a team, everyone should have the same vision. Your vision can be very clear and properly crafted, but if everyone does not embrace the vision, that will hinder your growth.

You have to be a part of the solution

In creating content, remember that you are helping customers to live a better life. Although you may create content, ensure that you are helping them solve problems and offering some kind of solution to their challenges.

Be objective

There is nothing wrong in being subjective when you are creating your content. When it comes to business matters, be objective. Do not take your staff's side when you know they are in the wrong, but because you share a bond with them you do not address a matter or a customer complaint.

In addition, when you receive feedback on your comment forms, view them objectively. In what ways can you take the feedback and positively make changes?

Be sincere

Do not say things just because you think you should say them. Do not exaggerate or go overboard with your words. People can see right through the charade.

If you have a customer who comes in, you can simply say, "You look lovely today," if you find she looks extra special. Do not exaggerate and embellish and use adjectives that would make your customers uncomfortable. People know when you are being cheesy and overbearing. Refrain from using pretentious tones. Remember that the purpose of content marketing is to enhance your customers' lives, so be honest with them and respectful. Their appreciation and glowing commendations will attract more people to your enterprise.

Conclusion

Thank you again for downloading this book!

I hope this book was able to enlighten you as to what you can do to improve your standing and integrity in your field of business and in content marketing.

Whether you have already started your business and wish to build your credibility, or whether you are new to the business arena, you have to dedicate the time to build your credibility. Devoting significant time does not necessarily mean that you have to spend large amounts of money to realize your goals. It is a matter of paying attention to the little things, hiring the right people, and ensuring that the people who work for you are properly informed about your business goals, products and services, and various marketing campaigns.

You should diligently market your content so that customers know vital information about the company history, your product or service, and the value of using it. You should also ensure that the people who work for you have knowledge about essential topics and are skilled in interacting with customers. They represent your brand.

There are various ways to ensure that your company is known for its reliability and integrity. Include statistics in your content. Rather than provide descriptions and generalizations, provide data to show that you are an authority on whatever particular topic you choose. Do not include irrelevant statistics just for the sake of having statistics. Your data should be pertinent and relevant to your discussion. Conduct your research properly and decide for which topic you will include statistics. It is not every piece of content that requires statistics.

Pay attention to customer reviews. Have forms on your websites so that your audience can share their opinions. You also have to examine your customer complaints and find ways to improve the value of what you are offering.

Refrain from exaggerating. Do not make daring and overreaching comments that will only leave your customers disappointed. Remember, the focus of content marketing is your customer. Inform the customers about the best qualities of your brand.

Customer service is very important, so ensure that your representatives are knowledgeable about the service or product that you provide, as well as the various marketing campaigns.

Conclusion

Once you implement these strategies, you will advance quickly in your respective field.

Finally, if you enjoyed this book, then I'd like to ask you for a favor, would you be kind enough to leave a review for this book on Amazon? It'd be greatly appreciated!

Thank you and good luck!

Other books by E J Scott

Email Marketing *(Beginner's Guide to Dominating the Market with Email Marketing)*

Email Marketing *(Strategies to Capture and Engage your Audience, while Quickly Building Authority)*

Email Marketing *(Tips and Tricks to Increase Credibility)*

Social Media Marketing *(A Beginner's Guide to Dominating the Market with Social Media Marketing)*

Social Media Marketing *(Strategies to Capture and Engage your Audience while Quickly Building Authority)*

Social Media Marketing *(Tips and Tricks to Build Credibility)*

www.ingramcontent.com/pod-product-compliance
Lightning Source LLC
Chambersburg PA
CBHW070227190526
45169CB00001B/106